100 YEARS OF THE BRITISH AUTOMOBILE RACING CLUB

GARETH ROGERS

The History Press

To my nephew Phil Rogers for the assistance to his low-tech uncle in the preparation of this book.

First published 2011

The History Press
The Mill, Brimscombe Port
Stroud, Gloucestershire, GL5 2QG
www.thehistorypress.co.uk

British Library Cataloguing in Publication Data.
A catalogue record for this book is available from the British
Library.

ISBN 978 0 7524 6180 9

Typesetting and origination by The History Press
Production managed by Jellyfish Print Solutions; printed in India

Contents

Foreword

My family's connections with the BARC go back more than half a century. I am particularly proud to have followed in my grandfather's footsteps as president of the club. As a child I spent many happy hours watching the racing alongside my grandfather in his old caravan next to the famous Goodwood chicane. Many times during our campaign to revive the circuit in 1998, I thought of the passion and determination he must have brought to the first opening of Goodwood back in 1948. At that time motor racing was just getting going again after the war and the BARC played an important part in establishing Britain as a world leader in the sport – a position it robustly holds to this day.

My family's close ties with the BARC have remained and seen us through some challenging times, both with the first Festival of Speed in 1993 and the inaugural Goodwood Revival. Thanks to the tireless energy and enthusiasm of both the management and the marshals, we have managed to create two events of which I believe the club should be justly proud.

My grandfather, himself a successful amateur racer and winner of the famous Brooklands Double 12, would be delighted to know that the club is still in rude health after 100 years. Back in 1952 Goodwood was the first circuit in Britain to stage motor racing after dark with the 9 Hours endurance race and the club continues to expand its horizons both at home and overseas.

As the first president of the twenty-first century, I am delighted to join this celebration of our club's centenary at a time when motor racing faces new challenges and new opportunities.

Charles March, 2011

Foreword

BY THE CHAIRMAN OF THE COUNCIL OF THE BARC, GUY WOODWARD

It is incredible to think of the BARC as 100 years old. From its formation in 1912 as the Cyclecar Club, its development into the Junior Car Club in 1919 to the BARC name in 1949, the club has an amazing history inextricably linked with the golden age of motorsport.

Last year I visited the museum at Brooklands where much of the BARC story is on display and it was a moving experience. This book documents much of the history of the club and its development over the years from its beginnings at Brooklands to its amalgamation with the Brooklands Automobile Racing Club and its base at Goodwood after the Second World War.

The association with Goodwood was of huge significance and although the BARC had to move its headquarters to Thruxton after 1966 due to the safety requirements imposed, it still has particular importance for the BARC. Lord March is our president and his grandfather before him, and the club runs his internationally famous events: The Festival of Speed and the Revival meeting.

The BARC has developed hugely over the years and is now one of the most significant forces in motorsport. It has proprietary rights over four of our most significant circuits, namely Thruxton, Mallory Park, Pembrey and Croft. We also have Speed Hillclimb venues at Gurston Down and Harewood. We run and own the commercial rights to the British Touring Car Championship and own the Motorsport Centre (the Ian Taylor Motor Racing School) which offers great experiences for people wishing to drive exotic cars on a race circuit. We also offer our expertise in running events across the world. We run at least thirty championships catering for all levels of competition.

Over the years many of the great champion drivers have driven at our race meetings and perhaps more importantly we have provided motorsport – at all levels, from the most junior to the highest level – to members of our club.

The BARC remains a members club and the council is made up of enthusiasts who are determined to maintain the great traditions of the club. We are not complacent but determined to continue the success story and add to the prestigious past of our great club, much of which is documented here.

We are acutely aware of the commercial, environmental and strategic issues ahead for the motorsport business but feel sure that we are well placed to deal with them and maintain the success that the club has enjoyed for so many years and also the unique club atmosphere that everyone involved with the BARC enjoys.

Now is the time for celebrating our centenary and I hope you will enjoy this book. At the end of year celebration when we raise our glasses I will also be proposing a toast to the next 100 years.

Guy Woodward, 2011

1

CYCLECAR CLUB

The night of Saturday 7 December 1912 was windy, dark and wintry. Astonished cottagers in the winding Surrey lanes ran to their windows and threw open their doors so that the soft glare of oil lamps and firelight splashed on roadside hedges and trees straining in the breeze.

Every few minutes, with a rattle and a roar, strange dark shapes flitted past their startled eyes down the slope between hawthorn and hazel. A procession of lights wound its way with squat black shapes silhouetted vaguely against the dim glare of white headlamps down the valley and up the far side past the woods. The long line of little red lights trundled over the ridge and, one by one, vanished from sight leaving on the night air the dwindling rumble of exhausts and the smell of burnt oil.

That night the good people of remote Surrey witnessed the conclusion of the first run of the newly formed Cyclecar Club as its thirty-odd members and their friends made their noisy way back to the distant glow that was London. An epoch had been marked in the history of British motoring and a club had come into being that was to leave many historic landmarks behind in its growth over the next century.

Within decades of motor racing being established at various circuits, if enthusiasts were to be asked: 'What is a cyclecar?', they would be quite unable to answer apart from perhaps a vague idea by some that such a vehicle was an early form of motor car.

The first motor club of all was formed, out of enthusiasm for the new sport of motor racing, in 1894 after an historic first motor run from Paris to Rouen. The following year the enthusiastic group announced their title as the Automobile Club de France. Two years later this country hailed the Automobile Club of Great Britain and Ireland which in 1907 became the Royal Automobile Club. Regional motor clubs quickly followed. The Midland Automobile Club had run their first hillclimb at Shelsley Walsh in 1905. Seven years later motoring had its first club dedicated to a special idea – the development and enjoyment of a new kind of motor car with the foundation of the Cyclecar Club.

A cyclecar was described at the time as a combination of the worst characteristics of a motorcycle and the more depressing features of a motorcar. However, there was to be almost fanatical devotion to the new kind of motoring that filled the gap between the two-wheeler (even with a sidecar made of basketwork and looking remarkably like a Bath chair) and the heavy, expensive and relatively powerful automobile that was the lightest of the light cars at the time.

To the undisguised hostility of the motorcycling fraternity who in the first decade of the twentieth century owed allegiance to the Auto Cycle Union, there was, in a branch of the Automobile Club, a growing demand for a hybrid between a motorcycle and a car. This was initially exemplified by the tricar. These machines had two wheels in front plus one behind taking the drive and seats in tandem. The passenger sat in front and the driver or rider perched behind, steering by swivelling the front end. The passenger's journey would be punctuated by having to leap out and push the contrivance up hills!

Then came the quadcar, a four-wheeler, still with the seats in tandem so as to retain the narrow track which was one of the attractions of the tricar to those who had narrow gateways or would house them in wooden lean-to sheds.

So, the demands for a small ultra-light car costing between £100 and £150 existed – The market for a cyclecar had been created. The cyclecar arrived soon after and following that came its official definition.

Archie Frazer-Nash.

The search was for something very light, lively, economical to build and operate with something better in the way of weather protection, even going so far as a windscreen and a hood. Many were working to that end by 1909. Among them was H.F.S. Morgan, champion of the three-wheeler. For the 'Gutty Morgan' as it was called, was a popular trials car of high performance and stability up to the outbreak of the Second World War. There was also H.A. Thompson and at a house in Hendon, Archie Frazer-Nash and Ron Godfrey were hatching a plot together. In France there was L.F. de Peyrecave and Robert Bourbeau.

While this activity was going on with one-off jobs that were appearing on the road, the journal *Motor Cycling* became interested in what appeared to be a development in their sphere but whether it was really a new kind of motorcycle with four wheels or a light car with a motorcycle engine was something that caused the editor, W.G. McMinnies, many heated arguments. Arthur Armstrong who was at that time editing *Cycling* had become infected by the atmosphere of enthusiasm surrounding those early days of automobilism and with eagerness joined 'Mac' in running *Motor Cycling*.

In the autumn of 1910 McMinnies was in Paris to cover the Paris Motor Show when he heard the crisp bark of a twin-cylinder engine and then saw a vehicle the like of which he had never witnessed. A wooden coffin, unpainted, on four motorcycle wire wheels, the top open and containing a man in front behind an engine and another, tandem fashion, with a steering wheel at the back. McMinnies took instant action and pursued the apparition and its occupants. In the vehicle was Robert Bourbeau. This was McMinnies' first close-up look at the Bedelia and from that moment he was a convert.

After that incident in France events began to move at an accelerated pace. Back in London, McMinnies poured out his enthusiasm, setting Arthur Armstrong alight for a start. Then he sought the directors of his firm. The new kind of machine which still had no name other than 'runabout' (to which H.F.S. Morgan stoutly adhered) was not, he said, a motorcycle, nor yet a car. It was not within the sphere of *Motor Cycling* nor the purview of *The Motor*. It was new, distinct and alone. It needed a new journal to focus and foster the enthusiasm that was bound to flare up when these machines began to come onto the market at prices well under £100.

By 27 November 1912 *The Cyclecar* was on the bookstalls with 64 pages measuring 11 inches by 8 inches. It had eighty-four advertisements between glossy covers at the resounding price of one penny apiece. Over 100,000 copies were sold at once.

As soon as it became known that the new journal was in preparation and as more and more vehicles were coming onto the roads, the Auto Cycle Union decided to adopt the new machines under their wing rather than allow the RAC to gain control – and new membership fees. A group was therefore assembled under the chairmanship of Colonel H.C.L. Holden who had supervised the plans for the building of the Brooklands circuit a few years earlier. Colonel Lindsay Lloyd, Clerk of the Course at Brooklands and an ACU committee member, came up with the suggestion Cyclecar and it was immediately adopted – the terms 'Runabout', 'Monocar' or 'Duocar' dropped into oblivion.

The next item on the agenda was to establish a definition separating cyclecars from light cars. Their decisions were forwarded to the ruling body of motorcycle sport – the Féderation Internationale des Clubs Motorcyclistes in Paris – and by the time that the cyclecar was off to record sales, the definition was promulgated at international level.

An advert for the Bedelia, the vehicle which so grabbed McMinnies' attention.

GROUP 1. LARGE CLASS.
Maximum Weight: 772lb
Maximum engine capacity: 1,100cc (International class G)

GROUP 2. SMALL CLASS.
Maximum Weight: 660lb, Minimum: 330lb.
Maximum engine capacity: 750cc (International class H)

The first edition of The Cyclecar.

Now that the movement had its recognition and in Britain its own journal, it was obvious that it should have its own club. By 1912 the cyclecar movement was booming; companies were being formed all over the country and there was furious hammering and welding to prepare models for the forthcoming October Motorcycle Show and wherever enthusiasts met, the talk was of forming a club. The initiative, however, came from an office in the Rosebery Avenue premises of the Temple Press where the *Cyclecar* staff were working energetically to prepare the first issue of the journal. In 1902 one of the founders of the Motor Cycling Club, the largest and most active in the country, was Ernest Perman. Once a racing cyclist, he had joined the firm to launch *Cycling* and was now General Manager. He put the suggestion to Arthur Armstrong and found it instantly snapped up. A meeting was assembled for a round-table exploratory discussion where, among others, were Frank Thomas, Osmond Hill, H.R. Godfrey, Glynn Rowden, W.G. McMinnies and Armstrong in the chair. The result was a decision to call an open meeting in London at the Holborn Restaurant on 30 October.

There were about sixty present that Wednesday evening at the venue which stood at the corner of Kingsway and Holborn. In the chair they voted the Revd E.P. Greenhill, who was chairman of the Competitions Committee of the ACU. It should be noted that at this stage the motorcycling fraternity regarded 'cyclecarism' as a branch of their own activities whereas the RAC was dubious about admitting the new machines to the dignity of their car world.

C.S. Burney (of Burney and Blackburn who manufactured motorcycle engines) proposed that a club be formed. This was seconded by F.A. McNab. The proposal was accepted with enthusiasm. When the meeting broke up, draft rules had been accepted and officers had been nominated for election at the inaugural general meeting at the Motor Cycle Show, Olympia, on 29 November. W.G. McMinnies was proposed as Club Captain, Frank Thomas as Honorary Secretary, A.C. Armstrong undertook to become Treasurer with Glynn Rowden asked to be Club Chairman. As club rules are the foundation stone of such an organisation, so a Rules Committee was appointed.

The inaugural meeting duly took place at Olympia with Glynn Rowden in the chair. Business was brisk. The subscription was fixed at one guinea with half a guinea for country members and the same for ladies. The proposed officers were elected en bloc and Osmond Hill agreed to help Thomas as Assistant Honorary Secretary. Between fifty and sixty joined on the spot – the Cyclecar Club was in existence.

Saturday 7 December 1912 was naturally a cold, wet and miserable day but some twenty cyclecarists, their passengers, their friends in real motorcars – a total of about thirty – were warm with eagerness and massive motoring coats. For this was the day of the first run of the Cyclecar Club. The plan was to go out through

Esher on the Portsmouth road to the well-known Wisley Hut Hotel fronting its wintry lake. The Revd Mr Greenhill invited all participants to tea afterwards at his Surrey home.

The men from *The Cyclecar* were there:

A motorbus turned round to look at us. Taxi cabs thought they should give way, sidling down to the kerb in their best Saturday morning style. A pair of equine thoroughbreds stood upon their hind legs and pawed the air with delight. A tram driver pulled up his house-on-wheels with such a jerk that the passengers were shot on the floor. A portly pedestrian, making his fourth attempt to cross Piccadilly Circus, bathed in the mud instead. Even the man on point duty put an electric light standard between himself and the perils of the streets. And then we passed.

The roar of the 8hp JAP swept up the torrent of abuse that marked our passage as we churned through a sea of slimy, yellow mud that made the heart of the stoutest taxicab driver turn faint. Not so the heart of our Duocar as we rocketed over the greasiest streets of South-East London. Beyond Putney we picked up a GN and, as one cyclecarist to another, hooted merrily, trod on the accelerator pedal and gave the glad-eye for a speed exhibition up Putney Hill. The GN, ebbing in the hands of some reckless young fellow, won easily and we considered as we picked up various cars one by one that their drivers were not looking too pleased about it. Later on the GN enthusiasts were discovered warming their hands by the roadside. So, hastily referring them to 'The Cyclecar Manual' and giving a nod to three gloomy-looking gentlemen in charge of a 'measured furlong' we made Kingston, Ditton and Esher without incident.

At Esher the GN came roaring by triumphantly. At 'The Boar' a Duo-ist was observed taking in a 'home fuel'. Presently, he too came to the front to give us an exhibition of skilful driving which we took to be a display of figure skating. At Wisley Hut there were already half a dozen arrivals besides an equal number of motorcarists who gathered round to gaze, awe-struck, at slackened belts resting in the mud. 'Aren't they awful?' said one. 'How they drive with belts hitting the ground beats me.' We informed him that we had the wind behind.

Every few minutes another arrival would perform the customary finishing sprint and brake test until there were nearly two dozen machines lined up at the roadside. These included five Duos, three GNs, three Humberettes, two GWKS, Parnacott's quaint-looking iron-clad, an AC Sociable, an Autotrx, an Averies, a Sherwin and a Bedelia besides several of the home-grown variety. Had there been an 'appearance prize' it would have been divided between Higgs (whose beautiful lilac-hued GN was almost spotless thanks to a neat arrangement of auxiliary wings) and the passenger who had been used as a mud shield on an experimental Duo. The front or back of whose head could only be made out by his overcoat buttons.

A Duo cyclecar.

Extended dash. disc wheels and other improvements carried out on the Duo. The D.A. cylinder (on step) and the Klaxon horn can be clearly seen.

Above: A GN.

Right: A GWK.

Opposite: The first edition of The Light Car and Cyclecar.

Some thirty members and friends sat down to lunch in an apparently very subdued frame of mind for was this not a very sedate and historic occasion? Only one lady member (there are two altogether) was present. Having been disappointed in the delivery of a new cyclecar, she had cycled down to the run. After lunch half the party followed the Reverend E.P. Greenhill's GWK over the Surrey hills in response to his invitation to take tea with him at Walton-on-the-Hill. Up, up, through winding lanes we sped with Thomas's big GN 'Hippopo-Thomas' scattering mud forty feet behind it and drowning all remonstrance with a bark that could be heard for ten miles. Keeping discreetly out of range we had a wonderful vista of a long procession of low-built, rakish-looking cars winding over the hills. Every now and then a dip in the road would shut out a view of the procession and then, far off, we would espy it once more speeding swiftly up the opposite slope.

A driving mist of rain swept across the country but what cared we as we tore over squelching roads with the crackle of a score of exhausts in front to guide our way and promise company at the journey's end? The spiritual joy of new motoring makes light of fleshly ills. It was dusk when we pulled up and joined the thronged tea tables.

Our last glimpse of the first run of the Cyclecar Club was of 'Hippopo-Thomas' roaring through the night silhouetted against the wide arc of its searchlight. Suddenly 'Hippopo-Thomas' threw up its back wheels and disappeared from view! It had shot across the main road and into the ditch on the far side! Fortunately it does not require a crane to haul a cyclecar out of difficulties and two lusty cyclecarists made light work of pushing 'Hippopo-Thomas' back on the road again. We let the big GN light the way, keeping to the sodden road with difficulty. Speeding north and homewards through steaming rain – damp, happy and thrilled with the joy of a wild cross-country drive. The Cyclecar Club had carried out its first run and made history.

That winter of 1912 the club had several evening social gatherings, for apart from driving cyclecars the members liked nothing more than talking about them. Already there was a distinct tendency for the membership to divide into two schools – the purist cyclecarists and the others who were looking at the new light cars with their admittedly better comfort and equipment.

The year 1913 was greeted with a Sunday run to Dunstable. Again it took place on a day of heavy rain over roads deep in mud. After luncheon there was an impromptu series of driving tests in the High Street and then a sort of hares and hounds road race across country for tea at Hatfield's Red Lion, during which it is reported that no one suffered belt slips in the steady rain, no one skidded off the road even when taking corners sideways and no one even broke down.

The year was marked by the club's first season of competitions opening in March with the first reliability trial from Oxford to the Cotswolds. This was the first event of the club that today stages major events in Great Britain. Nineteen competitors started.

The other feature of that year was the establishment of the club's series of hillclimbs at South Harting followed by a lobster weekend at nearby Selsey. The event, held on 28 June, was like all the other hillclimbs of the period up and down the country. It was the nearest that most clubmen could ever approach to road racing and was quite illegal.

As the police took no times over a measured mile – as was the custom when setting speed traps on the highways – there was no evidence that any of the cyclecars was exceeding the 20mph limit and for this reason no speeds were published with the results.

Even by the winter of 1913/14 a change was beginning to creep over the cyclecar scene. More and more light cars were coming onto the market and cutting in on cyclecar sales. Within the club there was a growing section of lightcarists drawn to the greater comfort,

silence and reliability of the little two-seaters available. The wave of cyclecar enthusiasm was on the ebb but not the enthusiasm of the club as a club.

Then, with their finger on the pulse of popular preferences, Temple Press Ltd altered the title of their journal to *The Light Car and Cyclecar* in October of 1913 with the accent on the former.

The committee of the club was now meeting once a month to cope with the business that was rapidly mounting, like the membership. In July 1914 among the elected members was Alfred Logette who became honorary legal adviser to the club, being a solicitor by profession, and remained in that capacity until the late 1950s. In that month too, Hugh P. O'Connell joined the committee and remained an officer, specialising in the technical side and acting as a chief scrutineer at race meetings for the next thirty years.

On 4 August 1914 war burst upon a startled world. The Cyclecar Club held no committee meetings that month of commotion but the officers met again in September. An examination of the minutes reveals that the only reference to what proved to be the most appalling conflict that had yet afflicted the civilised world (and was to continue for the next four years), was the fact that a member of the committee, commissioned into the forces, asked if he could remain on the committee for the duration of the hostilities. They then got down to planning a programme of rallies for 1915.

2

TRANSITION

The AGM was duly held in January 1915. It appeared that turnover had been £318, that there was £116 15s 8d in the bank, £1 14s 4d in the Treasurer's account and £1 15s 7d in charge of the Secretary. At the next month's meeting an important question was raised: was it not time to change the club title? This had been in the air for some time. Gradually the term 'cyclecar' had become almost derisory, for the days of the skimpy little machines with their clattering twin-cylinder engines and belt drives was being superseded by the true light cars and were now the refuge of sheer enthusiasts who still preferred their performance even at the expense of a wetting every time it rained. Various titles were suggested, out of which emerged, as the best of a poor selection, the 'Junior Automobile Club'. However, this was rejected by the RAC.

The necessity for change was seen to be forced on the club by the continued growth of the light car faction and it was quite clear that when the war at last ended, cyclecars would belong to the past and the light car had come to stay and develop. It was, however, pointed out that any such change would mean opening the club to owners of cars up to 1,500cc instead of 1,100cc and would likewise mean affiliation with the Royal Automobile Club at increased fees instead of the Auto Cycle Union.

The ever-increasing darkness of the war years, the mounting casualty lists, the ever-growing austerities and hardships of civilian life put such consideration into the department of academic interest. In April a general meeting suspended club activities and paid all funds into the War Loan.

There was, of course, no Motor Show that autumn. The club decided to have a show of their own, pressing on despite the disapproval of the trade. The new car rally took place in a field near the Red Lion Hotel in Hatfield amid a good deal of interest. Although in deference to the trade no price tickets were shown. The following day, Sunday, the entire rally moved to the Burford Bridge Hotel, Dorking, the scene of many club gatherings. On the Monday it set up the display again at Wisley, therefore exhibiting the cars north and south of London.

On 11 November 1918 at 11 o'clock in the morning sirens wailed and church bells rang. The Armistice had been signed by the German High Command in a railway carriage on a track through the forest of Compiègne and thus ended the long and terrible slaughter of four years.

The Cyclecar Club sat up, shook itself and as more and more members came home from the forces (although many did not return) – a reunion committee meeting was called for February 1919. Among those present was Arthur Armstrong, who had been running (and writing) three or four journals single-handedly throughout the war. It was revealed that the club possessed £100 in War Stock and in liquid cash a sum of £7. Recovering from this pleasant news, Armstrong recalled that the term 'cyclecar' had become almost a dirty word and that in any case if they were not on the way out, cyclecars no longer formed the backbone of the club. He therefore proposed that the title be changed and put forward his own idea of what it should be: 'The Junior Car Club'. They adopted this name from March 1919. The discussion was favourable and suggested that the four-wheeled members should affiliate with the RAC and the three-wheelers with the ACU. It was likewise agreed to set the annual subscription at one guinea out of which the RAC would claim their capitation fee and that a big drive should be opened to gain new members for which reason it was proposed to find a paid secretary or at least pay for secretarial assistance.

All this came up again at the first post-war general meeting in March held at the RAC's palatial premises in London and it was generally agreed that the club needed a new title. The RAC had rejected a suggestion of the 'Junior Automobile Club' possibly thinking that it sounded like a junior section of their own club. They fully approved of 'Junior Car Club' instead. They had also promised to form a light car sub-committee to which cyclecar members would be co-opted. The meeting fell in with all these schemes, agreed to divide allegiance between the RAC and the ACU – according to how many wheels the member owned – and passed the February proposals en bloc.

Now matters were on the move, the energetic committee meeting once again in April. Items on the agenda duly dealt with were the definition of a light car for club purposes, the advisability of adding 'Ltd' to the new title, the foundation of club branches in the provinces and the urgency of organising social events as rapidly as possible.

Sporting events were to include a General Efficiency Trial for absolutely standard cars, a club weekend at Brighton, the revival of the South Harting climb and the traditional weekend afterwards at Selsey.

As new members came in with motorsport experience, it was perceived that those who were devoted to the sport were beginning to regard the Junior Car Club as a must and it was the influence of these enthusiasts that caused the club's history to be bound up with motor racing in this country from that point on. At last, after much deliberation, the club defined the sort of cars eligible for their activities:

Light cars up to 1,500cc with four seats weighing at least 15cwt or up to 1,100cc with two seats weighing 13cwt.

Cyclecars up to 1,100cc with a catalogue weight for an open two-seater of 9cwt.

There were three other interesting developments that summer. One was that membership was steadily nearing 200, another that the club had become Limited and that the Exeter Motorcycle Club adopted the title Junior Car Club. This was an issue that aroused marked fury and led to a terse correspondence.

That October the committee decided to hold an annual dinner, the first to be held at the RAC in December. The dinner made a loss of £34, which had to be taken out of the funds then standing at £170. Not that it

Opposite: Professor
A.M. Low.

16

deterred the continuation of the event. At the committee meeting which discovered this unfortunate news, McMinnies suggested a big reliability trial should be organised in 1920 from London to Manchester. It was proposed for April, so that the weather should be neither too mild nor too tempestuous. Meanwhile the first General Efficiency Test was held on a road course with a series of ten tests – steering, reliability, petrol consumption, hillclimbing at speed, slow running, acceleration and braking, starting from cold, silence (where Dr Low's audiometer listened in), restart on a hill and general condition when all was over.

The 1920 club year was marked by the invitation to Sir Arthur Stanley, Chairman of the RAC, to become the first President. Dr Low was in the chair and in announcing the new President he reminded the audience that the promised light car and cyclecar sub-committee had done nothing very much and was now defunct. With Sir Arthur as a firm ally, he felt that the club's interests would be safeguarded.

Business at subsequent committee meetings proceeded smoothly with little of importance except that the Brooklands Automobile Racing Club were asked to include events for 1,500cc and 1,100cc machines in their programmes and the first provincial branch came into being in the north under the guidance of Dr Heiron. The year ended with a vigorous resistance by the club to the ACU proposal to take over the competition's control of four-wheeled cars over 1,100cc.

JCC members were not slow to attack Brooklands' records in the new light car class, officially recognised by mid-summer. A.G. Frazer-Nash took his GN up to the standing kilometre at 56.8mph and the mile at 56.2mph.

Archie Frazer-Nash at Brooklands.

Early in May the club held its first Members' Meeting at Brooklands where Frazer-Nash had been lapping at 76mph in practice. After the timed trials (which were obviously from a standing start) the first event was a race for monocars with two entries: Reggie Empson with an AV and Kaye Don driving a Tamplin. The race lacked thrills for the Tamplin had trouble on the way to the starting line and the AV cantered around alone.

The 1,500cc scratch race was won by Bedford's Hillman at 66.6mph. Next came a 1,100cc event – a duel between the partners Frazer-Nash and Godfrey with their GNs. Godfrey miscounted his laps and turned into the finishing straight too soon. When he turned round and rejoined the course the other was miles away and won at 54.7mph. Then came the 8.5 mile

Far left: Kaye Don and Malcolm Campbell.

Left: Aston Martin at Brooklands.

handicap, up to 1,500 cc with a proper field. The results were:

1. C.Finch GN 2 minutes 15 seconds start 56.7mph
2. L. Martin Aston Martin 45 seconds
3. G.Bedford Hillman Scratch

Excitement attended the one-make race for AV monocars subdivided into 750cc and 1,000cc, for the machines were naturally very evenly matched. Empson won the larger car class at 51.1mph, G.C. Houghton the smaller. The 1,100cc handicap became a GN race on account of non-starters and developed all the way into a battle between Finch and Godfrey in which Godfrey won by a length at 59.5mph.

The enterprising club had included a race for lady members in which there was a splendid duel between Mrs Frazer-Nash (GN of course) and

A Tamplin at Brooklands.

Top: The Eric Campbell car.

Above: Harry Hawker in a Sunbeam on the Members' Banking.

Miss Violet Corderey at the wheel of an Eric Campbell. They raced side by side until, on the last lap, Miss Corderey pulled out all the stops, slipped ahead and won by 15 yards at 49.7mph.

There was a 14-mile race with four starters and two finishers – the Hillman and the Aston Martin in that order, won at 74mph. The final event was a GN affair won by Mr Finch in the last 200 yards.

The JCC had indeed arrived into motor racing, for it was seen that with careful handicapping the minnows could compete among the titans with added excitement for the crowds.

In March of 1920 the club had taken a most important step in its career and booked Brooklands for a 200-mile race in October. That was, of course, the first big international race held at the track. It was a series that continued at Brooklands until 1928 and was staged later on at Donington and Aintree. New members continued to join in a steady trickle. As the 200 Miles Race drew near they included a spate of racing men among whom was a keen young man named Henry Segrave who was eventually to win the first Grand Prix for this country and become the first man to motor at 200mph.

The first London to Manchester Trial was held in April 1920 with an entry of forty-one. All but nine qualified for gold medals after completing the event without loss of marks, which suggests that the course was not too difficult. Also in 1920, *The Light Car and Cyclecar* put up a most handsome silver cup on an imposing plinth for the light car driver who went fast for one hour flat at Brooklands. This was promptly annexed by George Bedford and his celebrated Hillman with a speed of 78.73mph.

The club was advancing fast. A Southern Centre was formed in April 1921 – to become the South-Western Centre based in Southampton under the guidance of T.G. Hayter and the Northern Centre in Manchester was already finding its feet with T.C. Ormiston Chant as Secretary. More centres were envisaged in the Midlands, at Cambridge and at Exeter. When the year ended, club funds swelled to £2,000, greatly

Bookies at Brooklands.

assisted by a profit on the successful 200 Miles Race. It should be noted that competitors were required to pay entry fees of considerable amounts and that 'starting money' was quite unknown. Manufacturers raced for prestige and publicity and to improve their designs, while the majority of drivers were there for the sheer joy of motor racing. As a piece of organisation the 200 Miles Race in 1921 was a monumental success, largely due to the energy of Hugh McConnell. The motoring press were unanimous in their praise.

Although there was this accent on competitions and the reliability trials, the social side of the club was not neglected, although the response was not so numerous apart from the annual opening run to Burford Bridge Hotel near Dorking.

Early in 1922 the first permanent office was established in two rooms in the Lower Ground Floor of Clock House, Arundel Street, just off The Strand, at the inclusive rent of £130 a year for a three-year let. Percy Bradley was now the Honorary General Secretary and had the use of the smaller chamber for his own business purposes for £40 per annum. It was here that Bradley first suggested and then produced the Junior Car Club magazine: *Gazette*.

So in June of that summer the first issue of *Gazette* came off the presses to be welcomed by the membership with great enthusiasm for it was a most professional production. That issue had ten pages of text and ten pages of advertisements, plus four more comprising the front and back covers. It opened with a message from the committee which had now assumed the title of 'Council':

Above: Segrave's first long-distance victory.

Right: The Esso pagoda in the paddock at Brooklands.

In launching the 'JCC Gazette' the Council have but one object in view, namely, the furtherance of the interests of the club but they recognise that there would be little chance of the 'Gazette' achieving its object were it to follow the general humdrum lines of a parochial monthly magazine. It is intended, therefore, to keep its pages bright, readable and have permeating through it that personal atmosphere that should help in promoting the social side of the club's life.

The Council sees clearly that the 'JCC Gazette' can be a material help in identifying the interests that members take in the life and doings of the club. It can assist in bringing into closer contact the Centres, not only with each other but also with headquarters and above all it can prove a valuable missionary agent in procuring new members thus making the club an even stronger force than it is at present.

They have every confidence that the editor will make the 'Gazette' a source of interest and benefit to every individual member of the club, thus making the whole organisation a live, homogeneous and powerful body. – The Council

Second Members' Day, Brooklands.

At the Annual General Meeting, Frank Bale announced with some satisfaction that the club had £1,688 at the bank and that nearly 200 new members had been recruited. G.W. Lucas, Chairman of the South-Western Centre, asked for better representation on the Council, but after a vigorous debate withdrew his proposal.

Forty-four entries went in for the General Efficiency Trial. The event that had set a pattern for it included no frame breakers but put ordinary cars through a whole series of tests from braking to petrol consumption. On a bright March morning the trial started from the KLG factory at Putney Vale and after wandering through the Surrey hills, ended at Brooklands.

The Spring Members Meeting at the track followed in May with the usual programme of eleven smartly-run races of various kinds, including one for disabled drivers, and all, of course, on handicap.

The London to Manchester Trial in June ended in Albert Square, Manchester, where the competitors were welcomed not only by members of the growing Northern Centre but by the Deputy Lord Mayor and the Chief Constable. This indicated that the JCC moved among 'top people' even at long range from base.

Members were prominent as usual in many other club events. The most important hillclimb on the calendar was still the Midland Automobile Club's event on the private hill at Shelsley Walsh near Worcester, run at the end of July.

The club's great day, the 200 Miles Race at Brooklands was held on 19 August. This time there were to be two separate races. At 8.30 a.m. the 1,100cc class was to start and after a suitable luncheon interval the 1,500cc voiturettes were to be sent off at 2.00 p.m. Both classes were to cover 73 laps of the Outer Circuit.

On track at Brooklands.

For the first time a loudspeaker system was to be installed to keep the public informed of the state of the race in addition to the usual scoreboards in the various enclosures. 'One of the officials will talk from time to time into a receiver whence his voice will be carried to all parts, even up to a range of two miles.' This was to be effected, by courtesy of the *Daily Mail*, with an American Magnavox – the only one in the country.

At the subsequent Council meeting it was reported that there were rumblings of complaints from Weybridge residents concerning the noise of the racing cars, which had continued all day, but it was not until much later that the matter was taken to the courts and the 'Brooklands Silencer' was made compulsory. This was in the form of a large canister related to the cylinder volume and a final fish-tail on the end of the exhaust pipe.

The last important event that summer was the hillclimb at South Harting, where on a fine afternoon in mid-September over 1,000 spectators crowded the sides of the loose, dusty ascent and assembled six deep on the outside edge of the corners where any driver who lost control and slid would have certainly crashed into them. However, in this country at that time neither the officials nor the public realised the possible dangers of high-speed competitions. Three years later a spectator was injured during a similar climb at Kop Hill in the Chilterns. With the police restive, the RAC finally proscribed speed events on public roads, however remote.

3

NEW DIRECTIONS

Early in 1923 there was an expression of feeling among some of the non-racing members that the club was beginning to deviate from its original conception as a club for enthusiasts who wished to meet each other to talk motor cars and enjoy the occasional social run. There was at that time a great deal of discussion as to whether the club should open a country club. This gave rise to a letter in the *Gazette* from a member who was probably not alone in his views:

Suggestions for novel events appeal to all amateurs. Together wih friendly little social events such as dances which were what I, perhaps foolishly, expected when I joined the Junior Car Club. It appears our club has to choose between becoming a similar institution to the RAC or a jolly band of enthusiasts such as the Northern and Yorkshire Centres appear to be. Don't let the JCC fall between two stools.

The club was approaching, if not already at, a crossroads. Membership was increasing, chiefly among competitions enthusiasts. Should they continue to expand or remain static and dwindle? The Council deliberated most seriously along these lines, very clear in their minds that the rising influence of the JCC stemmed principally from the annual 200 Miles Race that had lifted them from the ranks of the general types of motor clubs into a position of national and international influence. The general feeling was that they must continue their destiny, for to halt now would mean stagnation and eventual decline. At the same time it was appreciated that the social side of club life should not be neglected but developed side by side with its progress in the field of motor racing. They knew that the old days of impromptu events and exhilarating runs through Surrey lanes had long passed; their cyclecars, whether they liked it or not, had grown up into motor cars.

As new members came in, the Council realised that club subscriptions no longer covered the rising overheads of the growing club. The crossroads had been reached. Now the sound finance of the JCC depended chiefly on whatever profit could be made from events in which the 200 Miles Race ranked of first importance.

Ready for racing.

Thanks to the 200 Miles Race, the JCC membership now included almost every well-known British racing driver, apart from a few who had no interest in 1,500cc racing at that time. The '200' of 1923 was run as one race with two classes – 1,100cc and 1,500cc. In the general category the winner was C.M. Harvey (Alvis) at the remarkable average of 93.3 mph.

In drawing up the 1924 fixture list, the Council again expressed its concern at the lack of support for purely social events and eventually decided to abandon the London to Manchester Trial which no longer attracted enough entries to make the heavy task of organisation worthwhile. However, the members cheered themselves up with a new club badge. This remained as standard for the next twenty years – a diamond with the words 'Junior Car Club' superimposed on an oblong plaque crested with the initials JCC.

At midsummer the Northern Centre, based in Manchester, became in response to popular demand the Liverpool and North Wales Centre. This embraced the territory of the older Centre under the leadership of Mr Phillpot.

The *Gazette* had now been appearing for three years and was well supported by its advertisers. The editor, Percy Bradley, printed his appreciation mentioning the staunch support of Palmer Tyres, Dunlop Tyres, Ferodo Friction Linings and Anglo-American Oil, who marketed Pratt's Perfection Spirit.

The 200 Miles Race that year was a gratifying success with a public gate of 8,681 with 1,450 cars plus 268 JCC members and the profit was £934 to swell the funds that stood at £2,800. For the first time the new 750cc cars were recognised with a class of their own – which resulted in eleven entries.

In January 1925 the Annual General Meeting was held for the first time in the salons of the Royal Automobile Club. Moving forward as ever, the club regarded the General Efficiency Trial as having fulfilled its original functions and replaced it with the first High Speed Trial for standard cars on a 100-mile course made up of part of the Brooklands track and the rest around the internal roads which were noticeably rough. The novelty of the competition, which offered what was practically a road race to members driving their everyday cars, attracted eleven 1,100cc tourers, twenty-two of 1,500cc and seventeen sports cars which were eligible only if they were strictly as per catalogue and if a reasonable number had been produced – a first attempt to define what became the Grand Tourer. At the same time, while on the

Below left: An Alvis.

Below right: Around the Brooklands banking.

subject of racing, for the first time three-wheelers were no longer eligible for the 200 Miles Race, nor for the High Speed Trial.

Meanwhile, an important and far-reaching idea was adopted for that year's 200 Miles Race. For the first time it was decided to erect an artificial corner to reproduce something of a Continental road race into an event at the track. This had never been done before but was extended and imitated in the years ahead. This time there was to be a barrier at the fork where the cars came off the long Byfleet Banking towards the flat right-hand curve past the Vickers factory. The drivers would then corner to the left into the mouth of the finishing straight, complete a U-turn halfway to the Paddock, return to the fork and corner left again to attack the steep Members' Banking. It was realised that this would reduce the lap speeds, but as the 100ft width of Brooklands dwarfed all speeds anyway then this loss was written off against the increased excitement of seeing the drivers cornering – something not witnessed before. The race was another JCC success. Nearly 11,000 paid for admission plus 365 club members, and saw a fine race. The winner was H.O.D. Segrave at 78.89mph.

Competitors race to their cars in the trial.

Reliability trial.

After all was over Malcolm Campbell wrote to the club:

I feel I must write you a few lines to heartily congratulate the club on the great success of the 200 Miles Race. I do really think that our club is to be most highly congratulated on such go-ahead methods and moreover the JCC has done far and away more to popularise motor racing that all the other organisations in this country put together . . . my one regret was the fact that I could not compete as I would have given anything to have taken part in this most interesting race.

The start of the 1925 200 Miles Race.

Above: Lining up for a race.

Up to this point, as one fan put it, 'Motor Racing was something that took place abroad.' During the winter meetings the Council pressed on with the plans for a JCC club room at Brooklands, proposed a long-distance race for what amounted to standard production cars on the Outer Circuit, deplored the apathy of so many club members and reported an attendance of 486 at the annual dinner held at the Connaught Rooms in London.

By 1926 there were now three major racing events on the calendar – the Members' Meeting in April, the Production Car Race in July and the 200 Miles Race in September. For the latter it was decided that mechanics should no longer ride with their drivers, therefore falling in line with the ACF Grand Prix ruling of 1925, although the cars were still required to carry two full-sized seats plus mirrors. One of the mechanic's duties, when they were permitted to ride in the car, had been to tap his driver on the shoulder whenever a faster car came up behind.

The club was becoming more and more a body of motoring enthusiasts and less and less a club for social runs with picnics, although several visits to factories and similar places of interest were organised.

Above left: Malcolm Campbell.

Above: Brooklands Automobile Racing Club – the original 'BARC'.

Above right: The P.A. system at Brooklands.

Now, as certain high-speed tuning and modifications were permitted in the standard car race, it was laid down that all the cars should be entered as 'Specials', so that any publicity afterwards would not be misleading to the public.

The new club room was opened at Brooklands, in the Paddock, that March. In July the High Speed Trial was duly run with forty-eight starters of whom twelve won gold medals. In a separate class labelled 'Specials', four more received special silver medals.

The '200' was now endowed with £500 as first prize and was run on an entirely new course, cutting out the Members' Banking. Segrave was a winner for the third time at 75.56mph. This was the best race of the series to date with a record gate of 10,853 plus 518 club members and 1,798 spectators in a special enclosure. The public address system, now with thirty-two loudspeakers around the enclosures and grandstand, operated through 12 miles of wire and were a great improvement. It is perhaps curious that the caterers reported a decline in the demand for beer.

The annual dinner, like the 200 Miles Race, proved the most enjoyable of the series. Over 600 members applied for tickets but only 498 members and guests were able to be accommodated at the Connaught Rooms in December.

When the AGM met in late January 1927 with fifty members present, membership stood at 951, producing a subscription of nearly £1,200, but the profit on the workings of 1926 was £130 down, owing to a series of steady losses. All of this suggested that the ordinary kind of event for the enjoyment of members who took no part in races where there was, of course, a strong trade element, reflected the lack of interest. This had already killed the Northern Centre which was disbanded by the Council at the first meeting of the year. Two steps were taken, however, to meet the club's situation. Two sub-committees were formed: one to handle competitions and the other to organise social events. This was undertaken in an effort to further the interests of both sections of the membership. On top of that it was decided to throw the club open to social members belonging to a full member's family, even if they possessed no car. The first of the new membership class was Mrs L.T. Hough – introduced by Mrs Hugh McConnell and therefore the club enrolled its 1,000th member in February.

As the Production Car Race had been something of a failure and with the original regulations seeming to lack appeal, it was decided to turn it into a Standard Sports Car race with, as was customary at that time, an entry fee of £5. In those days without entry fees no club could have financed a race at all. It was also decided to introduce yet another novelty (apart from the new club tie) in the spring meeting at Brooklands in the form of a Junior Grand Prix. The event made use for the first time of what became known as the Mountain Circuit – that part of the track which surrounded the Members' Hill comprising the finishing straight and the Members' Banking from the fork to the far end of the straight and therefore shaped like a letter 'D' and measuring 1.17 miles. So there were corners at each end of the straight but in addition an S-shaped chicane was set up halfway down the straight to add another. The Brooklands Automobile Racing Club was not slow to realise that once again the JCC club had started something and they were soon including 'Round the Mountain' at their own periodic meetings.

For the 1927 200 Miles Race in October, T.B. André added to his Gold Challenge Cup (for the entrant of the winning car) an additional silver cup for the designer. The former went to Malcolm Campbell and the latter to Ettore Bugatti. The race was a financial disaster. As expected by only having an October date available at Brooklands, the Motor Show in London drew off thousands of potential spectators. A somewhat gloomy Council brooded over the matter. It was decided not to ask for an international date for 1928. The season had been a poor one but the members flocked to the annual dinner.

The startline of the JCC 200 Miles Race.

Getting a good view of the action.

The year ended with the Council still pondering the future of the club. A small body for enthusiasts (which is how it began) or the largest and most influential club in the country? Was motorsport past its peak of popularity and already in decline? What was wrong in the Centres? Above all, what would happen to their finances if the 200 Miles Race was not held again or, if it were, made another loss?

The following year, 1928, opened with these questions still unanswered. There were discussions about opening the club to those with cars over 1,500cc. Membership stood at 1,123 – a net gain of 166, for 195 had resigned. At the AGM that January, eighty-six attended. T.G. Hayter wanted the club opened to bigger cars, retaining the light car limit only for competitions. Harry Edwards, a new councillor, supported this suggestion but went further asking for competitions open to cars over 1,500cc in racing as well as in reliability trials. Edgar N. Duffield, a well-known motoring writer, strongly disagreed: 'Why change the very thing that made the club in the first place?' The matter was left in abeyance, unresolved.

Frank Bale, Treasurer, announced that even after the poor year and with all bills settled – the funds stood at around £2,000. Other business included the opening of a social membership to people not owning cars whether they were of a member's family or not; the admission of big cars to competitions other than at Brooklands; and the formation of sub-committees to deal with RAC matters, technical affairs and election of members. Finally, another new idea was adopted – an illuminated member's badge combined with a rear light.

That April the club offices were moved from Arundel Street to Empire House, Thurloe Place, Brompton Road, where there was a ground floor for a members' room and offices adjoining.

In this year it was clearly seen that the 200 Miles Race was no longer the sort of event to attract a paying gate at Brooklands. A Special General Meeting was called that November when the Council announced its latest novel enterprise: a sports car race to be run for two days: 12 hours a day with the cars impounded for the night. It was to be a sort of 'British Le Mans' at Brooklands and with artificial corners. A straight

24-hour race was impossible on account of the restrictions concerning noise. The scheme was at once acclaimed. The only dissention arose when the Council suggested opening the event to cars over 1,500cc. In the end it was put to the vote and only four voted against the 'over 1,500' proposal but there was a clause: 'not at Brooklands unless it was essential to success.'

L.F. Dyer.

In December the foundation of the Double Twelve-Hour was well and truly laid. It was to be a race for sports or touring cars in full road trim, as at Le Mans, all of which were to be standard models as per catalogue, complying with the minimum weights specified in the International Sporting Code. The course was to be covered anti-clockwise, down the finishing straight, left onto the end of the Members' Banking, up the Railway Straight, round the Byfleet Banking, to the fork and left-handed into the finishing straight. It was also agreed that ladies could enter, but not as passenger-mechanics.

Two other events are of note that season. In the second week of September the club had organised a party to the Boulogne Speed Week and at the end of that month there was the first Night Trial from Virginia Water, Surrey, to Southsea.

In 1929 the Great Depression hit the country and unemployment ran into millions. However, at the AGM it was announced that membership had reached 1,318, a net increase of 219, making it the largest car club of its kind in Britain. At the meeting it was agreed that the Double Twelve race should be thrown open to cars over 1,500cc, but members emphasised that this was not to mean a lack of interest in light cars. The spring race meeting and the High Speed Trial had to be telescoped into one Members' Day in July as the Brooklands Automobile Racing Club, with more 'outside' races on its books, was forced to limit the free dates.

The Double Twelve was duly run on 10 and 11 May. It was based on a handicap formula relating expected performance to engine capacity so that merit would outweigh sheer speed. The race went to Giulio Ramponi, a well-known Italian engineer residing in Britain at the wheel of a supercharged 1,500cc Alfa Romeo two-seater with a speed of just 76mph. There were fifty-one starters. The club made every effort to create a Continental atmosphere at Brooklands with flags, bunting and even a complete fun fair. When racing finished on the Friday evening at 8.00 p.m., JCC members and friends had a party with a running buffet and dancing until midnight. The

THE BRITISH DOUBLE
TWELVE HOUR RACE
ORGANISED BY
THE JUNIOR CAR CLUB

OFFICIAL
PROGRAMME
1/-

FRI. & SAT. MAY 9th & 10th 1930
RACING 8-8 EACH DAY

second day's business began at 8.00 a.m. For some reason, possibly because there was very little publicity in the daily press which in those days headlined a motor race only when there was a fatal accident or something sensational took place, the Saturday crowd was not as large as had been hoped for. When all was added up there was a profit of between £400 and £500 gross.

However, new members were coming in every month and the leakage of resignations was plugged. From now on the club continued to grow steadily. At midsummer, Percy Bradley announced that Colonel Lindsay Lloyd, Clerk of the Course at Brooklands, was retiring and he, Bradley, was to take over that office at the end of the year. The Council, regretting but understanding this decision, appointed Leonard F. Dyer as General Secretary assisted by John Morgan.

As the year came to an end, plans were already laid for a second Double Twelve, to be held at Brooklands again. This time the performance handicap was to be replaced by a straightforward class handicap which the public could more easily understand and follow in so far as each engine size (on normal international lines from 750cc upwards) was set a minimum distance to be covered. The drivers exceeding this distance (or speed, for it was the same issue) by the greatest margin at any given moment were obviously leading the race. Tables in the programme could therefore inform the spectator how many laps each class should cover each hour at the handicap speed.

4

MOTOR RACING IS DANGEROUS

At the 1930 AGM the usual handful (fifty-one) attended the meeting. This suggested that there was very little criticism or dissatisfaction in the club. In March an entry of sixty-one had been received for the Double Twelve, already bearing the marks of success. Not so reassuring was a series of unfortunate incidents during the March half-day trial involving sightseeing motorists and cutting up of surfaces. Awards were decided by performances up to the point of cancellation and it was becoming more and more difficult to find a suitably interesting trials course near London, for local residents were complaining about trials by a variety of motorcycle and car clubs taking place over the same hills week after week.

The Double Twelve was staged in May. As a race it was a great success with a magnificent entry ranging from 6.5-litre Bentleys, 3-litre Talbots, 2-litre Lagondas, Alfa Romeos, Alvis, Lea-Francis, Aston Martins and Frazer-Nashes down to Rileys, supercharged MGs and Austins. It was sadly marred by a disaster toward the end of the first day's racing.

Two Talbots had been racing in line ahead, perhaps a length apart, but as they came down the finishing straight towards the turn onto the banking at the end (taking the circuit anti-clockwise) the slip-streaming car collided with the one ahead. Both cars crashed but one reared into the air and tore through the spiked railings of the public enclosure opposite the pits and into the crowded spectators. Several were killed, many injured and one of the riding mechanics died. The tragedy threw a black pall of gloom over the event. The race eventually went to Woolf Barnato and Frank Clement (6.5-litre Bentley) at 86.68mph.

The June Inter-Centre Rally was won by the Yorkshire members with London as runners-up. There were forty-three starters. The tenth Southampton to Exeter Trial likewise drew poor support after which the organisers, who were beginning to outnumber the competitors, came to the conclusion that an easier route might attract more entries from members with their everyday cars. On the other hand the Members' Day at Brooklands in July attracted fifty-nine entries. Among the gold medal-winners in the High Speed Trial was the young Earl of March in his first event. He was eventually to become club president as the Duke of Richmond and Gordon.

The September issue of the *Gazette* scored its century: a record for any club magazine. In the winter there was a demand within the club to revive the 200 Miles Race for 1,500cc cars, vigorously supported by Malcolm Campbell. The big cars admitted to the Double Twelve were overshadowing the light cars and were far removed from the original aims. The majority view was that the club must move with the times, and very few 1,500cc racing cars existed to form a field that would draw a crowd. It was pointed out that in spite of the tragic accident of the Double Twelve, the club, dependent on its racing programme for its financial security, had made a profit of over £900.

A very important suggestion put up to the Council by Bunny Dyer was seen immediately to have great possibilities. This was to run a 'handicap race on scratch' at Brooklands. The idea was to start the field from scratch in groups of cars of theoretically equal speeds and then to split them up at a series of channels or artificial corners. Side by side at the fork but of differing severity so that the small cars would go through a full-throttle curve and at the other end of the scale the fastest cars would have to cut speed for a slow turn. Something between the two would confront the medium-sized machines. If the precise angle of these channels was worked out correctly, the lap speeds of the entire field would be brought to equality, near enough. It had

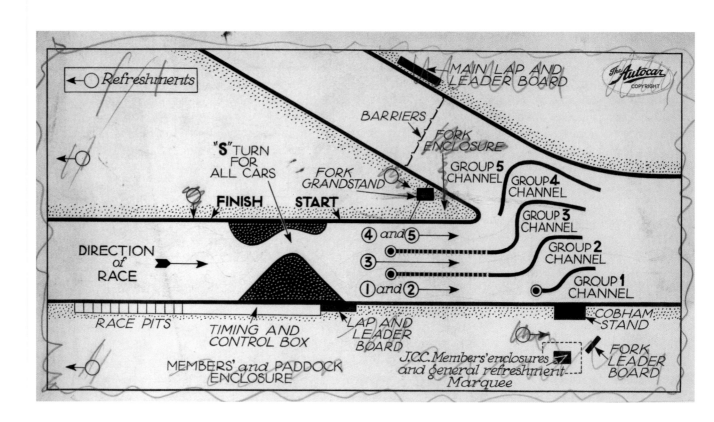

The channel system at Brooklands.

never been done before but the JCC was famous for its originality and such a race should surely appeal to the crowds for, in spite of the disguised handicap, the cars out front would be leading the race as if on scratch. A committee was appointed to examine this enterprising scheme which in principle it enthusiastically supported.

It was also decided to press on with the organisation of a third Double Twelve in 1931 with the proviso that no success was to be advertised to the public as being won with a standard car. As at Le Mans, permitted modifications in the pursuit of performance were definitely non-standard in relation to what was printed in catalogues.

At the 1931 AGM there was a proposed Thousand Miles Race which was to replace the Double Twelve in 1932. A two-day race again, but on time handicap so that all cars would be set the same distance. The club was also now coming to the reluctant conclusion that there was so much traffic on the Saturday roads that the days of light-hearted race days was over and Sunday events were abhorrent in this country.

It should be noted that this was the year that HRH Prince Chula of Siam joined the club. In the years immediately ahead he became one of the best-known figures in British motor racing as patron of his cousin, Prince Bira, to whom he presented a new ERA 1,500cc racing car on his twenty-first birthday in 1935 after which 'B. Bira' became a star of international light car racing.

Entries poured in for the Double Twelve. By the end of April there was an excellent field, even if the foreign element was meagre. In the event it would appear that the handicappers had somewhat underestimated the pace and reliability of the MG Midgets, for these little machines scampered home at the end of the second day with Lord March and Chris Staniland first in 65.6mph. The cars were also second, third, fourth and fifth.

Prince Bira and mechanic.

The July Members' Day with the High Speed Trial was a record with eight events run off like clockwork during the afternoon. Each had forty to fifty entries. The streamlined organisation of the volunteer JCC officials was already established as a model – a reputation which has endured until today.

The September Night Trial was again a success and in October the South Western Centre's Lynton Trial, which replaced the Southampton–Exeter, was likewise a success. The year ended with 500 present at the annual dinner, which was a record for any motoring club in spite of the Depression that still hung over the country like a black cloud.

Lord March at Brooklands.

New plots were being hatched concerning the Thousand Miles Race. The cars were to be sports cars but in racing trim less lamps, hoods and wings: three items that at least would not be shaken off on the notorious bumps of the Brooklands track. Riding mechanics were to be optional and three men could work on a car at the pits. The race was to be 200 laps (500 miles) each day, starting at 10.00 a.m. each time but now running in a clockwise direction – the normal international way.

There were signs of consternation at the AGM of 1932. The Secretary announced that for the first time in ten years the membership had fallen. To attract more members, a special reduced subscription was introduced at 25s for owners of small cars, up to 10hp on the RAC rating, carrying with it full RAC touring benefits.

An indication of the times was, perhaps, a letter in the *Gazette* pleading for scratch racing on the grounds that handicaps killed the interest and made the racing impossible to follow for the ordinary spectator who paid at the gate. The problem was, of course, that in all sportscar racing, the fields varied from cars of 750cc up to over 7.0 litres and there were not enough equal-sized cars to make a race on their own except in short-distance races.

Arising out of the frightful accident in the 1931 Double Twelve, an action was brought in the King's Bench Division of the High Court before Mr Justice McCardie and a special jury in March. It was argued for four days. The plaintiff was a Lt. Hall, suing the Brooklands Estate Company, Mr Arthur Fox (entrant of the Talbot team) and the two drivers involved – Hebeler and Rabagliati – for injuries sustained. Lt. Hall claimed that the spectator protection was inadequate and that there had been negligence by the drivers and others. The jury in the Brooklands case were out for three hours. They found for the plaintiff against Brooklands Estates, owners of the track, in a sum of £950 plus £38 expenses but not against the entrant or drivers of the Talbot. Leave to appeal was granted and there was much discussion in court concerning the risks that spectators accept in watching a motor race. After that signs were erected and admission tickets were printed with the warning: 'Motor Racing is dangerous'.

Meanwhile the search for some alternative to Brooklands went on (there were no available aerodromes then) until at last the Derby and District Motor Club secured Donington Park a few years later.

A month before the Thousand Miles Race the prize fund had reached the point that made all the difference between profit and loss for the organisers. The prospect of prize money was the only financial inducement for entrants whose entry fees were an important factor in the final balance sheets and for this the club had to depend on the generosity of others.

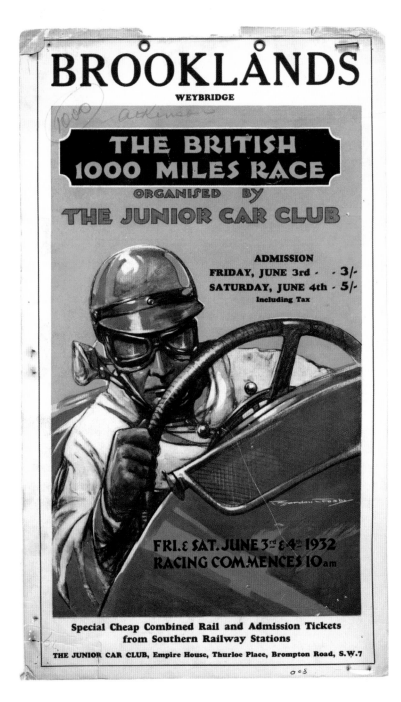

Mrs Wisdom and Miss Richmond in a Riley finished first on handicap. There had been loud criticism of the handicapping prior to the race, despite the fact that the Handicap Committee had slaved for seventy-eight hours over the task. However, the finish was close with all seven finishers on the same lap and the speeds were higher than the handicap so there cannot have been very much amiss in the pre-race calculations.

Then news arrived that the Brooklands appeal had been heard by Lords Justices Scrutton, Greer and Slessor who reversed the decision in the lower court and awarded the Brooklands authorities costs in both courts. This was not only satisfactory for the winners but it put a stop to a whole spate of lawsuits that were pending on the result of this case. The matter hinged on whether the safety precautions had been reasonable, having regard to the established fact that no car had ever crashed into the enclosures in the previous twenty-three years of the track's existence and it was also established that the crowd attended at their own risk.

Moving on there was a letter from 'A new member' in the *Gazette*: 'What is wrong with motor racing . . . is that it has never been a national sport and never will be. A rich man's hobby for those who can afford the best car and best mechanics win. The man in the street takes no more than a passing interest in motor racing. . . .' There was truth in this point of view and it was becoming more and more apparent that whereas racing at Brooklands was thrilling for the competitors, the 100ft width of the track and the remoteness of the action was

Above: Miss Richmond and Mrs Wisdom after the 1932 Thousand Miles Race.

Above right: A front view of the channel system.

inclined to bore all but the knowledgeable enthusiast. Road racing had yet to come to England but the Tourist Trophy thrilled the Irish spectators year after year and drew 100,000 to its 13-mile course where 99,000 could stand behind fences and hedges and watch it for nothing.

As the year drew to a close and the twenty-first birthday loomed up, the Council hinted at yet another novel event for 1933 to add to their long list of original competitions – a new 24-hour trial and an increase in social acivities, such as parties to attend races on the Continent. A caravan section was formed, the winter dinner-dances and the film show continued while the sixteenth annual dinner was held again at the Connaught Rooms. Then at last the Council announced the 1933 International Trophy, 'the scratch race on handicap' where each class would have its special corner and the field would be funnelled safely into them through a chicane in the finishing straight.

5

COMING OF AGE

With the twenty-first year of the club's history, the JCC may be said to have moved into modern times. The immediate success of the new International Trophy with its ingenious handicap corners, the support it received from the trade and its popularity with the public put an end to the old long-distance handicap racing with its admitted monotony and difficulty of following its progress except with elaborate lap charts and stopwatches. So a new era of racing began in Britain where real road racing was soon to be shown to the spectators for the first time at Donington.

The sign of the changing times came when the Derby club sent an invitation to stage a JCC meeting at their new D-shaped circuit in the wooded parklands of Donington Park owned by Mr J.G. Shields of Derby. A circuit of 2¼ miles had been made from existing roads, running at one point through the farm buildings and at another under a somewhat narrow stone archway in dense woods but with a half-mile straight which had been used by racing cyclists then by motorcyclists. However, at this stage the RAC had not approved the course for car racing. It was therefore suggested that members might accept invitations to compete in the Derby club's own events for the time being.

Although entries were flowing in for the International Trophy, there was little interest on the part of foreign drivers. Indeed only Count Stanislas Czaykowski had sent an entry for a 2.3-litre eight-cyclinder Bugatti. The *Gazette* wrote:

> There can be no doubt whatever that the list of racing events at home and abroad is fast outgrowing feasible limits. It is laid down internationally that no two classic races should occur within two weeks of each other but this period is insufficient to permit really satisfactory entry lists to be secured in every case. The fact remains that we are hemmed in by events abroad and thereby robbed of the appearance of many important people. Any British event is already handicapped because of the expense involved by foreign teams or individual entrants coming so far to participate.

This was true. Apart from which Brooklands was unsuited to road racing cars and had developed cars of a special nature. Indeed, few manufacturers were interested in racing at all.

The race was an outstanding triumph, voted the finest yet staged at Brooklands. The handicap corners did what was expected of them while the crowds could see and understand what was going on without recourse to complicated tables. It was reported as a fine sight to see three cars dash side by side towards their appointed channels and corner, parallel with each other but at very different speeds then accelerate out the other side, still in much the same order. The winner, after just under three hours of racing, was the Hon Brian Lewis (2.3-litre Alfa Romeo) at 88.07mph by 11 minutes 15 seconds in 250 miles. The club had proved that the new handicapping worked and promptly secured the exclusive rights in the method for some years ahead. No other existing course possessed the great width of the area of the fork where the channels were set up.

The channel system in action.

Once again, as in the days of the Cyclecar Club, members began to raise their voices to suggest another change of title. Junior Car Club, they declared, suggested a small-car club devoted to light car activities. Indeed it once was, but now they were an influential body staging for some years the most important races in the country, open to cars of any capacity. The old arguments were trotted back and forth but the question was side-stepped at least until the 1934 AGM.

The coming-of-age celebrations took place on 8 December in the ballroom of the Park Lane Hotel, London, at the annual dinner when 644 applications had to be reduced to 500. The guests were received by Dr Low and Mrs H. Hill, the wife of one of the club's earliest members. Colonel Moore-Brabazon proposed 'The Club' to which Dr Low replied.

So into 1934. Motorsport was at last on a rising wave of popularity all over Europe after the dull years when the Grand Prix had fallen into the slough of Free Formula racing with few entries. Now, however, a new formula was in operation for cars weighing not more than 750kg but with engines of any size that would come within that weight limit. This had the effect of bringing back Mercedes into racing together with the new Auto Union – a product of four German factories – to race against Alfa Romeo and Maserati of Italy, and Bugatti of France. Voiturette, or light car racing, was reinvigorated by the advent of the ERA built at Bourne, Lincolnshire, in Raymond May's workshops set up in the grounds of his house. English Racing Automobiles, ancestors of the later BRM, were built for sale to any buyer, much as Bugattis were but at the same time there was what amounted to a factory team.

The Donington circuit was in full service. Brooklands was as busy as ever and the Continental Grand Prix followed one another at monthly intervals. At the AGM it was announced that Sir William Morris had promised another £500 for the International Trophy and that the race would be run on much the same lines as before but would be open, not by invitation, but by election from among the applicants and there would be a slight regrouping of the cars within the three classes. On the last Saturday of April the International Trophy was run again. The race ended with just 4 seconds between Whitney Straight, the winner, with a 3-litre eight-cylinder Grand Prix Maserati and the runner-up Brian Lewis on a similar model at 89.62mph and 89.59mph respectively.

It was agreed that the main event for 1935 should be the International Trophy again and that the suggestion of another Double Twelve, a Standard Car race or a 24-hour race on the Isle of Man or anywhere else were not practicable.

Early in 1935 it was plain that members were joining in a steady flow. The days when the numbers fluctuated had long since gone and when the AGM was called that January it stood at 1,877, an increase of 184. There was a surplus of £287 on the 1934 activities and there was the comfortable sum of £3,315 invested and earning interest. Among items on the agenda was the decision not to run a proposed Manufacturers' Trial before 1936 as the idea was fraught with complications. Most clubs continued to run into the difficulty of defining a 'standard car'. Just the same, the club decided to ask the RAC for a permit for possible future use. Another item was a discussion on the possibility and desirability of forming a Midland Centre and another was correspondence with the Derby and District Motor Club concerning a race at Donington as suggested by Cecil Kimber of MG.

Then it was announced that the International Trophy would be held on the King's Jubilee Bank Holiday, 6 May, and this time the entry would be divided into four classes with four separate handicap channels. The trophy prize fund had risen to £1,150 by mid-March and passed £1,500 a month later.

There were now nine special committees in addition to Council meetings every month dealing with Events, the International Trophy, Technical, Races, Finance and General Purposes, Social, Election of Members, Caravans, Legislation and Traffic.

The International Trophy that year was, up to that time, the most successful race the club had organised before a big crowd that returned the largest financial gain the club had ever made (in May the funds were standing at £6,447). The race was won by Luis Fontés, a new name in motor racing and English, driving a 2.3-litre Alfa Romeo at 86.9mph by 2 minutes and 28 seconds.

The next racing event was a meeting at the new road circuit in Donington Park at Castle

Raymond Mays in R4D before the 1938 '200'. R.G.J. Nash's vehicle behind.

Raymond Mays.

Donington between Loughborough and Derby. This was at the invitation of the Derby and District Motor Club. It marked the first racing venture of the club outside its historic stamping ground of Brooklands, where it had already revolutionised the old idea of track racing. There were two circuits at Donington at that time. One was the distorted D-shaped course of just on 2½ miles. The other, offered to the club for this experiment, was an inner circuit of just under 2 miles and very fast indeed. This went straight on after the pits instead of turning sharply left at Red Gate corner and ran for almost a mile parallel with the return straight but with only one slight bend about halfway and a semi-circular turn at the top end. This was the first time the shorter circuit had been used. It had been built primarily for the smaller club meetings and for midweek testing. Admission to this event was half a crown with free parking and there was an entry of forty-four sports cars on that 31 August. The meeting, with eight races for cars in full road trim, was a sporting success but a financial loss – around £80. However, the event had been good publicity for the club in a new area and out of subsequent discussion arose the suggestion of reviving the 200 Miles Race for 1,500cc cars in 1936. More and more wealthy young men were buying ERAs and modern voiturettes existed in France and Italy as well.

Later that year the old controversy started again about the club title but the general consensus of opinion was that any alteration would be a mistake in view of the fact that the initials 'JCC' were too well known and had long outgrown any association with little motor cars.

At the AGM in January 1936 the Secretary announced a membership of 2,012. Although he had recently resigned as Chairman of the Royal Automobile Club, Sir Arthur Stanley confirmed that he would continue as President of the JCC for the fourteenth year. The gathering was also informed that the club intended on 2 May to organise the International Trophy again on the lines that had proved so successful but to split the entry through five, instead of four, handicap channels. In addition, the classic 200 Miles Race was to be revived, this time at Donington on 29 August as a scratch race for cars of any size. There would be separate awards in the 1,500 class. The June Members' Day was to be run at Brooklands. The Inter-Centre Rally at Leamington and the Evening Trial were both in the fixture list again.

The International Trophy of 1936 went down as one of the finest and closest races run at the Brooklands track. The last half of the 261-mile struggle became a tense duel between Prince Bira and Raymond Mays, both in 1,500cc ERAs. On the last lap they swept off the banking into the finishing straight almost together. Bira streaked for the line precisely one second ahead of his friend at an average of 91mph. The timekeepers gave May's average as 90.99! There was, to the relief of the club, a fair financial return but by no means what had been hoped for. This was reversed at the close of the season at Donington where the JCC slice of the cake was four times bigger for a start.

That same month, largely due to the energy and enthusiasm of Frank Bale, the club added the Midland Centre operating in Warwickshire and around Birmingham to the existing three with D.B. Welland as Honorary Secretary.

The feeling about the title was becoming deeper and more widespread, especially among those Centres. A special meeting, called for 8 June, debated the matter all over again and all the old arguments were tossed back and forth with vigour. What was disliked was the idea conveyed by the word 'Junior' but not a soul present could think up a better idea. There was 'Junior Automobile Club', 'The Car Club', 'The Motor Club of Great Britain' and 'Car Club of Great Britain'. Nobody liked any of them. At last the matter was put to the vote. Eight opposed change, nine wanted it, but with the proviso that some acceptable designation should be found and none of the suggestions so far made should be adopted. There the matter was allowed to rest and it was resolved that in the meantime the well-known initials should be used alone rather than the full title. The 'Junior' part of it should be played down at all times.

Prince Bira at the ninth '200', at Donington in 1936.

Above: *R. Seaman (Delage) wins the 1936 '200' at Donington.*

Above right: *The pits at Donington.*

The eagerly-awaited 200 Miles Race was staged on 29 August at Donington on the full Grand Prix circuit. There was no handicap. The race was open to single-seaters of unlimited capacity, for there were not as yet enough modern '1500s' to make a full field on their own without an influx of foreign cars and drivers. They, accustomed to the receipt of starting money, were discouraged by the expense if not the distance.

There was an assembly of twenty-one cars and the race was a personal triumph for a new driver – Richard Seaman. Seaman was driving the straight-eight Delage which had been raced previously by Lord Howe and it was Howe who challenged Seaman all the way in an ERA.

The owners of Brooklands had not been blind to the popularity of road racing ever since the JCC showed a kind of road race could be staged on the track, but the success of Donington, beginning in 1934 and the first Grand Prix of 1935 and underlined by the revival of the 200 Miles Race, helped them to decide to construct a road course within the perimeter of the pear-shaped track. This was completed in 1937 and named after the now-knighted Sir Malcolm Campbell. The new road turned off the Railway Straight just beyond the swoop down from the Members' Banking, made across the flat infield towards the fork, crossed the finishing straight, ran back parallel with it and then curled round the foot of the members' enclosure with its trees and emerged on the beginning of the Members' Banking. The JCC at once negotiated and got the assurance of 'special consideration' in the use of the circuit when it was completed.

At the 1937 AGM there were New Year greetings sent by many leaders of the motor industry, signalling the twenty-fifth year of the club's life. In more mundane matters, reports showed a surplus of £390 for 1936 and funds standing at £5,320 with a membership still going up at 2,117.

The International Trophy went off at Brooklands on August Bank Holiday with another JCC innovation – a rolling start for the entire field, rank on rank, for one lap behind John Cobb at the wheel of the famous 4-litre V-12 Sunbeam with his foot well down. The club had introduced massed starts years before, a method that had now become commonplace. So it was thought proper that something new – and practical – should be demonstrated. Raymond Mays with a 1,500cc ERA bored out to 1,980cc led from start to finish – pursued by Prince Bira's 3-litre Grand Prix Maserati, until it broke down. The attendance was a bumper one and the satisfactory result was a surplus of £375.

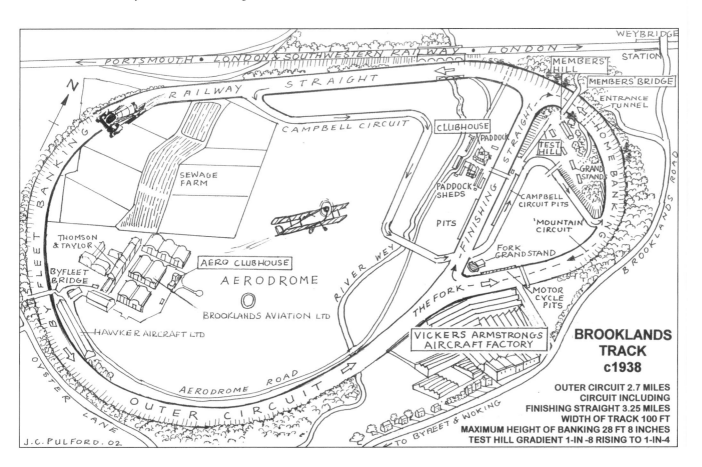

Three weeks later the club was at Donington again for the 200 Miles Race. This was the tenth of the historic series that began at Brooklands back in 1921. The racing was first class with a magnificent battle between Raymond Mays and Prince Bira again, until Mays fell out. Arthur Dobson (ERA), who had won the Prix de Berne 1.5-litre race the Sunday before, swept into the fight. He passed Bira and when Mays' ERA snapped a halfshaft with only thirteen laps to go, automatically took the lead and beat 'Bira' to the line by just under 40 seconds.

Going into December, when the Centres were organising their annual dinners, social activities, film shows and dances to conclude the first quarter-century of the club's history, the Council decided to organise the same two major races again in 1938 – the International Trophy at Brooklands, this time in May, and the 200 Miles at Donington in the last week of August. The storm clouds were gathering in Europe but low down on distant horizons. There was foreboding but the race-organising clubs drew up their 1938 programmes and left these anxious affairs to the politicians.

Dobson in the pits at the 1937 '200' at Donington.

Business at the AGM was, as usual, mainly formal, which probably explains why only some fifty to sixty members ever attended. When it was learned that the new Campbell Road Circuit at Brooklands was to be ready on time, the JCC with their usual alacrity, at once booked the course for the next 200 Miles Race instead of Donington. However, there was to be a Members' Meeting at Donington again.

For the second time a hideous accident took place in a JCC race which could not have been foreseen and almost at the same spot as in the Double Twelve tragedy. A new circuit was used for that year's International Trophy on 7 May. This was a combination of the new Campbell Circuit and the main Outer Circuit plus the finishing straight. Just as the flag was raised for the start, it was seen that under the pointed tank in the tail of the Frenchman Joseph Pall's big V-12 Delage, little tongues of flame were hungrily licking. Before anyone could move (and drivers in the row behind were shouting) the flag fell and they were away, rank on rank of twenty-three roaring cars. Paul got around the U-turn at the end and realised his predicament. Gradually he edged the Delage out of the ruck and onto the flat grass verge at the foot of the bank on the left. A.C. Lace, behind him in a Talbot, was caught unawares by the car's sudden loss of speed and change of direction and slammed into its tail. Instantly the blazing car turned at right angles, plunged up the bank, killed Murray Jamieson, the racing car designer who was standing there, and ploughed into the spectators ranked along the pathway at the top. Ten people were injured, one fatally.

Arthur Dobson (ERA) winning the 1937 '200'.

Eventually Percy Maclure in a Riley won after Raymond Mays lost one cylinder and Prince Bira had his back axle chewed up. Both had been leading at one point.

The attendance was not up to expectations and in spite of the fine racing a loss was seen to be inevitable. Now all depended on the success of the 200 Miles Race in September. Whereas there were now three road circuits including Crystal Palace plus the ordinary Brooklands Outer Circuit and Mountain Racing – public interest was waning again. In these circumstances the club began to consider alternatives for the following year. It would be unacceptable to continue writing off losses in a club where the ordinary income from subscriptions did not meet the administration costs and the subscriptions could not be raised without losing

*John Cobb and Reid
Railton at the Bonneville
Salt Flats.*

members at once. It is probable that more than half the membership joined the club to go motor racing, most of them active competitors.

The new Midland Centre staged a meeting at Donington with the utmost enthusiasm and efficiency. The racing was good. The attendance was not, however, and the Centre sadly reported a loss of between £60 and £70 – a considerable sum for a small body in those days.

A meeting of all race organisers was called for the end of September for the same malaise afflicted all alike – Brooklands Automobile Racing Club, the British Racing Drivers' Club, the Derby club with its Donington problems and the new club at Crystal Palace in addition to the JCC. The situation was discussed without arriving at any conclusion on what action could be taken. All agreed, though, that the lack of support from the factories who had abandoned official racing, and lack of money, except from outside and infrequent sources, were the roots of the problem.

The JCC decision was to suffer not more than a £500 loss over the year but to press on in 1939 with the International Trophy early in May. They also considered a possible second race which might or might not be the 200 Miles if the funds could stand it, and to apply for full international status for both events through the RAC. It was also decided that this was no time to start forming a centre in Bristol. Even the annual dinner and dance was cancelled for lack of support – the first time in many years.

On the brighter side of the picture, however, was a successful Venice Rally which brought thirty-eight members and sixteen cars safely home after being wined and dined by the Dutch, German, Italian and Swiss Automobile Clubs.

So towards the end of that August the eleventh 200 Miles Race was back again at Brooklands, but on the full Campbell Circuit of 2.26 miles. The expected renewal of the struggle between Mays and Bira came to nothing when Mays retired after only fourteen laps. Bira's 2.9-litre Maserati produced brake fade and left Johnny Wakefield to win at 70.97mph in an ERA. The attendance was good, but the probability of another small loss was accepted.

All this time the political situation was growing steadily more menacing, although most people thought war could not possibly happen again.

The twenty-sixth annual dinner was held at the Park Lane Hotel in London with nearly 500 at table. Among the many celebrities present were members George Eyston and John Cobb who had duelled for the World Land Speed Record, scoring one each that autumn.

Then the great title question came up again at the December Council meeting and this time nine voted for change, unopposed, with one abstaining. The new title was to be recommended to the 1939 AGM as 'The British Motor Club'. The Council felt, 'that the words "Junior Car" are a deterrent to further progress and that under the suggested title "The British Motor Club" membership could be more easily increased and the club's influence in the motoring world extended.'

The Annual Meeting met with about fifty members present to discuss the matter and did so at some length. The majority agreed that 'Junior Car Club' was outmoded and misleading but the Council's proposal of 'British Motor Club' was felt by most to be a little grandiose, if not pompous. No one had any better suggestion and the problem was left open so that members who were not at the meeting could send in their solutions (out of which a generally acceptable title might yet be discovered). As a matter of fact it was not until about ten years later the question resolved itself when the Brooklands Automobile Racing Club was wound up and the famous initials taken on by the JCC.

Meanwhile the Secretary reported that the Centres had regained vitality and both South-Western and Yorkshire had surplus to show. By May there were 112 new members. The Brooklands Rally was again oversubscribed and was run with 146 entries. The London competitors won the shield from Liverpool in the Inter-Centre Rally at Cheltenham and there were twenty cars with forty-five occupants entered for the second Canadian and American Rally.

On 6 May the seventh International Trophy was run on the same course as in 1938 but with only three groups and three handicap channels at the fork. The accuracy with which these had been laid out was remarkable, for the first three cars to finish were all in separate groups and all on the same lap. The crowd was about one-third larger than in 1938 and the day ended with about £500 for Frank Bale's coffers bringing the funds up to £6,000. It was then decided not to risk dropping money on the 200 Miles Race which was accordingly cancelled together with the Midland Centre meeting at Donington. The Brooklands Members' Day, however, was run with all its customary success although the entry for the High Speed Trial was smaller.

On 3 September the stormclouds over Europe broke. At eleven o'clock on that Sunday morning, Neville Chamberlain went to the microphone and sadly informed the nation that Britain was at war with Germany. Half an hour later the first air-raid warning sirens wailed out across the country and a chapter of history was ruled off, for nothing was ever quite the same again.

6

BRITISH AUTOMOBILE RACING CLUB

A week after war was declared a Council meeting was called at the Waldorf Hotel in London after which the club's affairs were put into cold storage for the duration of the conflict. All activities ceased. The club's records were put in store, the offices were sub-let and it was proposed to suspend the *Gazette* which they presumed could not be carried on without sufficient advertising revenue, and the Council predicted an immediate cut-back on the part of the trade. Actually, this did not take place to the surprise of the management of all the motoring journals. It became obvious that the motorists who could no longer motor, except within the narrow limits of petrol allowances for essential business, were all the more eager to escape from the tensions of wartime by reading about the pastime that was now denied them. The *Gazette* was therefore kept going as a bond between the 2,320-strong membership, although at quarterly intervals. It was edited by John Morgan.

Members were still paying their subscriptions and a kind of club life still existed, if mostly on paper in the *Gazette*. The elders of the Council who had already fought one World War and were engaged in a second – but not militarily – did their best to keep in touch, for they were practically the only members who could. In this Frank Bale was the prime mover, instigating a series of luncheon meetings that gradually became organised into fixed monthly functions to which guests were invited as and when available on leave from the forces and from industry when time could be spared. These happy gatherings blew a breath of sanity through the wartime nightmare and it is certain that those few who could attend kept the JCC alive when it might so easily have disintegrated.

It is clear from the volumes of the *Gazette* how little was then foreseen of the future of motor racing. In Britain it had always been a Cinderella among the sports. There was little or no factory support and no factory teams. The public was generally apathetic regarding racing as something that went on behind the high walls of Brooklands, while the national press looked on it as a source of news only if anything sensational occurred and not as a sport worthy of inclusion in their back pages. Writing in 1943 Sir Malcolm Campbell gave his opinion that there would be no international racing on the Continent and that no racing cars would be built for many years after the war had ended. In point of fact there was motor racing in Paris within a month of the end of the war and all over France within a year. Britain entered Formula 2 Grand Prix with an entirely new team of HWM 2-litre cars within five years, new Maseratis appeared in Formula 1 and motor racing attracted bigger crowds than had ever been known not only abroad but in Britain where it was encouraged by road circuits springing up all over the country.

At the end of January 1944 a General Meeting was held in London with about thirty members present for the first time since 1939. Frank Bale took the chair in the absence of Dr Low. The accounts were adopted with enthusiasm and congratulations to the Council and officers who had kept the club in existence at so small a financial loss. George Peachey proposed the re-election of the Council en bloc which, seconded by A.F. Rivers-Fletcher, was passed unanimously.

As that fateful year slipped into history there was a new feeling in the air that could be described as a kind of anxious optimism. Along with other similar bodies, the club was stirring again and the Council was planning tentatively for the revival of club life. There were misgivings concerning Brooklands and Donington Park, though. The former was almost unrecognisable with buildings on parts of the track and the old concrete overgrown with grass and young trees which had thrust up through the broken surface. Brooklands had never been a fruitful investment for its shareholders and now it began to be conjectured that the historic track might be sold as it stood to the Vickers aircraft concern who had taken it over during the war. Donington was an Army vehicle depot and inevitably destroyed as a racing circuit. Its owner, J.G. Shields, had died that May at the age of eighty-six. Even if the War Office could be persuaded eventually to release their grip on the park, it was doubtful whether the new owner, Mr Shields' son, would have the same enthusiasm for motor racing or the large sum of money available that would certainly be needed to reconstruct the circuit and its essential installations.

The Council, looking to the future, decided to launch a Motor Sport Fund for the sole purpose of re-establishing the sport in Britain. On 5 September 1945, for the first time since the war, a cocktail party was held to mark the re-union of the club. In this happy and crowded atmosphere Frank Bale made the first public announcement of the British Motor Sport Fund and its objectives. From then on cheques began to come in fast until a £2,000 mark was soon reached and passed. Very wisely the Council made no specific announcement as to how the money would be used apart from its general purpose, preferring to wait on events.

Later that month the RAC called a conference. It was an informal meeting with no minutes and no agenda, open to representatives of all motor clubs. This was intended to air views and survey the new scene. It was greeted with satisfaction as a sign that the governing body was anxious to broaden its outlook and to come up to date. The RAC made it clear that they were aware of difficulties ahead such as the fate of Brooklands and Donington, the problem of the supply of tyres for competition and the general desire to restart motorsport as soon as possible.

In Council Gordon England suggested that a disused airfield might be a possible venue for a race meeting or a speed event of some sort. So began a serious search for somewhere to race. Next came the important proposal by C. Gordon Bennett of the Jersey Club that the JCC should undertake the organisation of a road race at St Helier. The Jersey authorities, he said, had been approached and were favourable to the scheme. The Council were immediately interested and arrangements were made for a party to inspect the proposed circuit and, if suitable, to obtain the first refusal on the staging of a race at as early a date as possible. Matters were beginning to move. Now a club office was needed again as the lease at Empire House had long since expired. John Morgan had been conducting business from his own home but as affairs reverted quickly towards normality, this was no longer practical. Frank Bale stepped into the breach and offered an office in his own business premises. So 1945 ended and the club was back in business.

The first post-war season was of paramount importance in the life of the JCC. At the AGM His Grace the Duke of Richmond and Gordon was elected President of the club. Then forty-two and still in RAF uniform, he was pondering far-reaching enterprises in the realms of motorsport. Frank Bale, now elected Chairman, recalled that as the Earl of March, 'Freddie', as he was known to all his friends, had won the Double Twelve in 1931 driving an MG Midget with Chris Staniland. In 1948 the duke was to complete the Goodwood circuit near Chichester just below the wooded downs of his estate for the exclusive use of the club, therefore founding its position as the most active race-promoting body in the country.

The major discussion centred on the recent news that Brooklands had been sold and the Brooklands Automobile Racing Club wound up. That March a committee was formed to go into the question of a takeover bid for that club or what remained of it. It was discovered that when war broke out it had 1,275 members of whom 700 had continued to pay a nominal annual subscription of a guinea which was to be refunded by Brooklands (Weybridge) Ltd. The committee suggested that these members should be invited to join the JCC and hand their refunds into the Motor Sport Fund.

An informal discussion took place at which the Duke of Richmond and Gordon presided between Bale, Dyer and Morgan for the JCC and Sammy Davis with Percy Bradley for the Brooklands Automobile Racing Club. As all of them were members of both clubs, then everything was amiable. Now once again the question of changing the Junior Car Club for something better had come up. It was immediately seen that a new title lay ready to hand retaining the historic significance of the Brooklands Automobile Racing Club initials but with one word altered. The JCC was to be the British Automobile Racing Club: a title that explained exactly what the club had become. It was decided to register the title immediately.

The Events Committee, back in action and delighted to have any events to think about, met in April and registered their opinion that the club should engage in no events at all unless they were of a first-class standard and on a closed circuit or course. They set their faces sternly on any kind of competition on the public roads while petrol rationing continued.

That winter the customary annual dinner was not held – this was still the era of rationing and little cards which entitled the holders to so many points for the purchase of little luxuries. Instead a buffet-dance was organised at Park Lane's Grosvenor House towards the end of November and no fewer than 600 tickets were sold.

It was realised by both the JCC and the BRDC that if a race was to be staged in this country it would have to be on a circuit of their own finding. In this the JCC was in the lead, for the Jersey Road Race

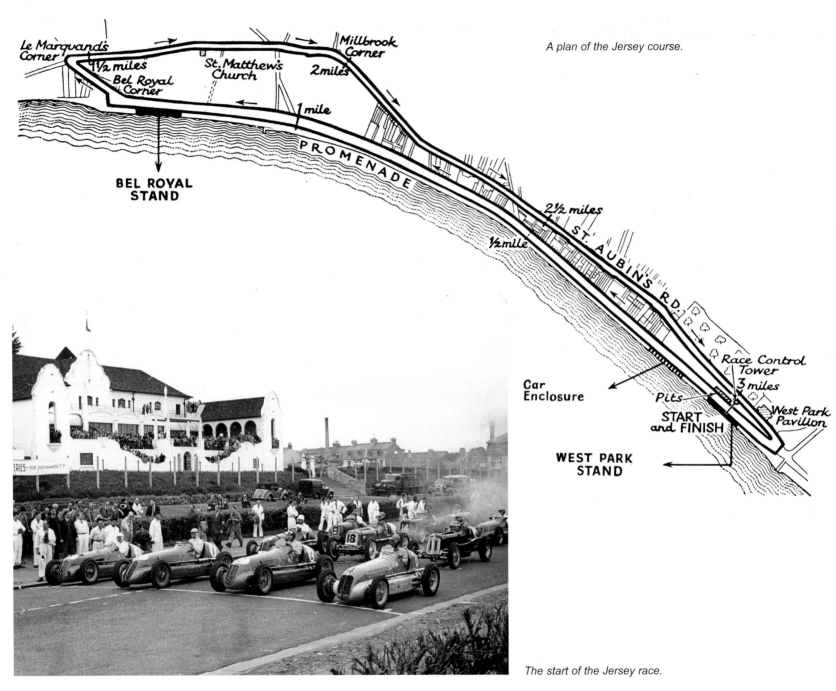

A plan of the Jersey course.

BEL ROYAL
STAND

WEST PARK
STAND

Car
Enclosure

Pits

Race Control
Tower

3 miles

START
and FINISH

West Park
Pavilion

The start of the Jersey race.

St Helier, 1947.

Prince Bira at Jersey in 1947.

was scheduled for May of 1947. While it did not bring racing to the English public it at least offered an outlet to British drivers and was calculated to present a new spectacle to the islanders which the Jersey Tourist Office regarded as important to their economy, first as publicity and secondly as a tourist attraction. Early in 1947 the necessary processes of law were accomplished, the Privy Council signed and the Royal Assent was obtained for the closing of the St Helier road circuit. The first Jersey Road Race organised jointly by the JCC and the Jersey Motorcycle and Light Car Club took place on Thursday 8 May.

The circuit, which ran alongside the bay and formed a hairpin inland to return through the streets and downhill to another hairpin, measured 3.2 miles to the lap. This was to be covered fifty times to make about 160 miles. The lists were opened to racing cars up to 1,500cc with superchargers or 4.5-litres unsupercharged. Prizes in trophy and cash value totalled £1,000. The public were asked to pay 5s to enter the course, a guinea to enter the steel scaffold grandstand opposite the pits on the promenade and 10s to park a car alongside the circuit.

Eastbourne sea front.

The club staged the Jersey race with great success as an event but it was financially disappointing. In all there was an entry of twenty-five cars with Reg Parnell (Maserati) winning the race. The financial loss of £1,000 fell not on the JCC but on the Jersey club and its guarantors in accordance with the agreement. Just the same, the Jersey enthusiasts were not deterred and immediately asked the club to organise similar events in 1948 and 1949.

The first post-war affair for members other than the racing drivers involved a weekend at Eastbourne with a rally in which ninety-one cars took part and a Concours D'Elegance with fifty-nine entries on 28 and 29 June.

In August 1947 something took place that changed the entire future of the club. The President, the Duke of Richmond and Gordon, invited the Council to visit his disused Westhampnett airfield within a mile of the beautiful horse-racing circuit on the crest of the wooded downs to the north. Here, using the winding perimeter road, the duke planned a course which would measure 2.4 miles. Negotiations still remained to be concluded with the various ministries who had interests on the site, but the duke believed that there would be no real problems and that there could be an experimental meeting sometime in 1948. The club officials withdrew impressed, not least by the duke's eagerness that only the JCC – soon to become the BARC officially – should have the right to organise the racing. The future of the retitled club which had come a

long way since the wire and plywood cyclecar days began to clarify and was full of promise for the years ahead.

The Jersey race was discussed at the first Council gathering in January 1948. It was agreed that the race should be run under the new International Formula which admitted cars up to 1,500cc with supercharged and up to 4.5-litres without. It was a formula that covered the prewar racing cars from 1.5-litre ERAs up to 4.5-litre Talbots and all the versions of the 1.5-litre Maserati. Racing fuel (methanol and the like) was available and the Ministry of Fuel kindly agreed to supply petrol coupons for the use of officials in connection with the race. The date agreed was for 29 April.

The Jersey Road Race listed twenty-eight entries of whom twenty-one took their place on the starting grid. Bob Gerard from Leicester (after whom the first bend at Mallory Park was eventually to be named) took his well-prepared ERA 'Old Faithful' into the lead and stayed there to the end.

New members were pouring into the club which elected the 2,001st in May. It was obvious that General Secretary Morgan needed proper office accommodation. Up to this time Frank Bale had provided a room in his own business premises but the work was outrunning the space. In July the secretariat moved into a suite of rooms on the ground floor at 55 Park Lane, London, fronting Hyde Park. This was on a share-the-rent basis with the Order of the Road and everybody was happy, for the new offices were worthy of the rapidly growing prestige of the club.

On Saturday 18 September, which was a great day in the annals of the club, the first Goodwood meeting was held. Member Denis Berry, a director of Kemsley Press, presented £500 and a handsome trophy. Entries poured in for selection as at this experimental meeting only twelve cars were started in any race.

The Duke of Richmond and Gordon opened the circuit in his new Bristol and in the cavalcade that followed was Tommy Wisdom in his Bentley. It was Tommy who had planted the seed of the Goodwood circuit in the duke's mind and Tommy seized it himself from Wing-Commander Tony Gaze whose brother flew on his last mission from that very airfield satellite to Tangmere.

Jersey result and advert.

Goodwood circuit plan.

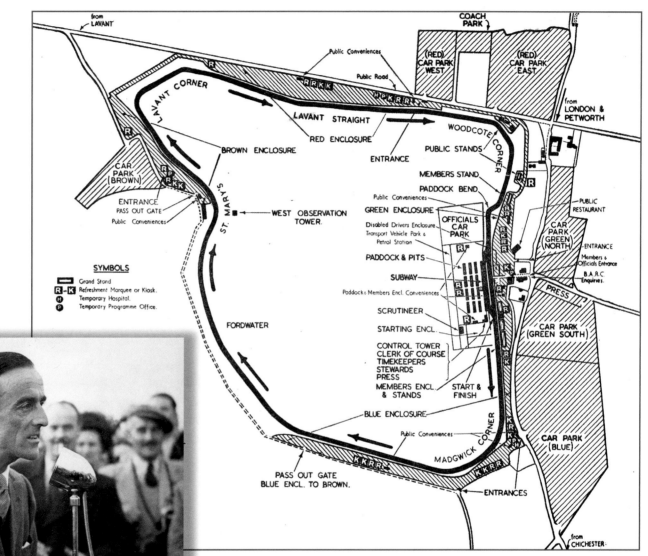

The Duke of Richmond and Gordon officially opens Goodwood in 1948.

Above: *The Duke of Richmond and Gordon drives his Bristol to officially open the Goodwood circuit.*

Queues form for the launch of the new track.

There were no grandstands, no pits nor paddock buildings but hastily improvised enclosures had been roped off at a safe distance and over 15,000 spectators managed to get there and into them. Every race had a massed start from positions drawn by ballot. Every race was, in the club's tradition, run off precisely on time. There were spins and skids and one overturned car all executed in complete safety and no serious accident marred the great day.

F.C. Pyecroft with a special Jaguar '100' had the distinction of winning the first race at the new course. Stirling Moss (500cc Cooper) began his brilliant career by winning his race and the finale, although the Goodwood Trophy went to Reg Parnell and his new Maserati which was making its first appearance in the

The pits in 1948.

Above left: The first race at Goodwood.

Above: Reg Parnell receives the Goodwood Trophy from the Hon. Denis Berry.

Left: Reg Parnell leads Bob Gerard in 1948.

country. In a five-lap duel with Bob Gerard's pre-war ERA, Parnell averaged 80.6mph to win by a short length and in his efforts Gerard set up the first circuit record at 83.4mph.

The Goodwood opening was a complete success although it was by no means a summer day. At the gates 10,478 paid their money and about 1,000 members flashed their badges. There were 108 entries for the eight races and 85 of them actually raced. The drivers liked the track. Sir Stirling Moss recalls, 'This was an excellent circuit. It was much trickier than people realised but you could make up time in various places. Lord March was also so hospitable.' Kemsleys, who put up prize money, liked the whole affair and the duke resolved to go ahead in building grandstands and installations for the future. Goodwood was on the map.

The club had already absorbed the rump of the prewar Brooklands Automobile Racing Club with the idea of preserving, in some measure, the traditions of that historic body. Now that Goodwood existed, the atmosphere of Brooklands could to an extent be captured in the post-war years – the memory of Brooklands and all it stood for would be recalled by the adoption of the famous initials. No fewer than 150 members went to the January 1949 AGM principally to see the matter through as item seven on the agenda. Alfred Logette moved the change of title to 'British Automobile Racing Club' seconded by Captain Archie Frazer-Nash. After some debate about alternative names, the title was adopted by eighty-eight for and forty-one against. The new BARC was in business.

Stirling Moss' first ever race victory, Goodwood, 1948.

Other business produced a strong plea for plenty of sportscar racing at Goodwood as distinct from single-seater and Grand Prix events. It was arranged that a delegation of keen sportscar men should meet the Events Committee to discuss a programme.

Of note were the tributes, warmly and sadly paid, to the memory of Sir Malcolm Campbell who had died aged sixty-three a few weeks earlier. He had been a member for many years and brought lustre to the club by his remarkable achievements. He held the World Land Speed Record nine times and was the first man to drive at 300mph. He held the Water Speed Record at 141.7mph. At Brooklands he was one of the great champions and won the JCC 200 Miles in both 1927 and 1928.

Feverish work now went on at Goodwood to prepare for the first international meeting on Easter Monday, 18 April. Members plus North and South stands overlooked the curve into the final finishing straight. There were enclosures at Madgwick corner and beyond, and a stand at the end of Lavant Straight with a

Early facilities at Goodwood.

view of Woodcote, the last corner. There were spectator enclosures overlooking the start-finish area and the paddock beyond, at Madgwick, at the curves through St Marys and along Lavant Straight. There were also two car parks with one opposite the main gate and the other for access to Woodcote Corner.

The Kemsley Press Group again offered to support the Goodwood meeting and also the Jersey Race coming up ten days later on 28 April. The Goodwood Easter Monday meeting was an almost frightening success. A crowd of a size no one expected invaded the enclosures, for many hundreds, perhaps thousands, made their way to the course by entries other than pay-gates.

The main races of that afternoon both went to Reg Parnell and his new 4 CLT/48 1,500cc supercharged Maserati. The racing was thrilling and close throughout the seven events with just enough spinning off onto grass to bring gasps from the packed thousands, and it was all run off with that spot-on timing for which the club had an envied reputation. Even with the uninvited non-paying guests, the day was financially successful as well as an achievement worthy of the club's long history of race organisation.

Two days later the duke convened an emergency meeting to plead with the Council that the proposed Whitsun meeting should be cancelled. He urged that present arrangements for public control could not possibly cope with the kind of crowd that they might expect. The circuit needed more fencing and stouter protective barriers for the enclosures. He foresaw the possibility of a major disaster if a car plunged out of control away from the track toward the spectators. The Council, who were there that Easter Monday, saw the weight of the duke's reasoning and the meeting was abandoned. It was promised that all additional safety measures would be taken in good time for the final meeting planned for 17 September.

There was barely time for these deliberations before the club was busy on the Jersey Road Race on 28 April. The second day of practice brought tragedy when Kenneth Bear was killed as his Bugatti went out of control and with him died a police sergeant and a local doctor who were standing on the side of the road where the car crashed. In the gloom that overcast St Helier that night, the stewards decided the race should go on the following day.

The weather could not have been worse. The start was put off for half an hour until visibility permitted motor racing at all. The awful conditions played havoc with the gate although those locals who made it were rewarded with a magnificent display of skill as the cars tore by in dramatic clouds of spume. It was a day of triumph for the modest Bob Gerard (the 1948 winner) and his trusty old ERA. He defeated the Continentals to win at 77.1mph nearly 3 minutes ahead of de Graffenried in his Maserati.

Steadily and rapidly the membership now began to move up to the 3,000 mark. Dixon Cade, son of Laurie Cade, a veteran motoring journalist, was appointed assistant to John Morgan while there was another vacancy for a helper to look after the growing needs of publications, printing and publicity. Next arose the

Goodwood mishap and rescue, Easter Monday 1949.

important matter of a new badge to replace the simple and well-loved diamond of the JCC. A prize of £25 was offered for the best design. Within four months, artistic and imaginative members presented over 350 sketches. While this profound problem was nearing solution the first Members' Meeting was duly staged at Goodwood on 13 August with no fewer than 104 entries confined to owners of sports cars. Nine races were run off with precision on a glorious afternoon of warm sunshine and if the handicappers with no post-war data at their command were now and then somewhat confounded, the drivers made up for it with many close finishes of an unexpected nature.

The racing season was concluded on 17 September with the Goodwood meeting in fine weather that brought the spectators in their thousands. Stirling Moss marked his twentieth birthday by winning the opening race at 82.1mph with a 998cc Cooper Jap and Reg Parnell driving his twin-supercharger Maserati broke his own lap record twice, first at 87.6mph and then at 89.26mph.

In December the winner of the £25 award for the selection of the winning badge design out of 375 sketches was Basil S. Smith of Hove, Sussex. He was a twenty-four-year-old student at the Brighton College

Jersey street racing.

of Art. It was in the shape of an heraldic shield bearing the initials 'BARC' vertically down the left-hand side, a fluttering chequered flag of victory as a background and a rampant British lion looking suitably savage and stamping its feet while brandishing its paws. That Christmas, 2,970 motorists were entitled to fix that new badge to their cars.

7

NEW CIRCUITS – NEW OPPORTUNITIES

With the dawn of 1950 the pattern of the club's activities steadily expanded as the years rolled by until they embraced the bienniel organisation of the RAC Grand Prix of Great Britain in 1955. Of course the club was firmly established for the future with the base of their existing operation at Goodwood. The structure of the Goodwood annual programme was crystallised as three major meetings – at Easter, Whitsun and in September, plus three members-only meetings in May, June and August. The main event for non-racing members was the Eastbourne Rally and Concours which had won the wholehearted support of the Eastbourne Corporation and the enjoyable Continental rallies continued to attract full support.

A scheme was adopted for an annual social programme to consist of a film show in October, the annual dinner and dance in November, the informal dinner and dance in December with another in January. A film show was scheduled in February and for the non-racing but competitive members, a night trial in June and either a gymkhana or a trial in August.

Next came the reorganisation of the administration of the Centres. The South-Western group ceased to be entirely self-governing in financial matters with these to be handled by London HQ. A social committee was formed to run local events of that nature but the events under the RAC permit were to be mainly a London responsibility. As for the Yorkshire and Liverpool Centres, subscriptions and badges became HQ matters but local finances for social and sporting events remained their own affair. HQ were to lend all assistance with printed matter and circulars to members. Therefore there was now to be one set of records covering the entire club, maintained in London.

On Whit Monday the club again broke new ground with the first classic race for the 500cc cars. The race was run in two seven-lap heats (there were forty-nine entries) of about 17 miles each and a final of 15 laps, 36 miles. The final went to Doug Dryden in a Cooper by less than a second at 77.2mph, Peter Collins was second and John Cooper himself third, all in Coopers. The races, in accordance with 500cc practice, were unleashed with a rolling start for one lap behind Sydney Allard, the reigning hillclimb champion in an Allard Cadillac. It was a novelty that appealed to the crowd.

An Eastbourne test.

The fourth Jersey Race was held on 13 July. It ended in a magnificent duel between Reg Parnell (Maserati) and Peter Whitehead with the first 1,500cc twelve-cyclinder Grand Prix Ferrari seen in this country, who finished first less than 5 seconds in front at 90.9mph. In fact the first five drivers to finish all averaged a higher speed than the previous fastest race in 1948 and David Hampshire broke the lap record at 94.93mph with his Maserati. The event was a resounding success as a spectacle but was rather less satisfactory financially.

An equally spectacular event, if of a different kind, was the first Midnight Concours D'Elegance in connection with the rally at Eastbourne. The novelty was that the lady passengers were required to act as models, walking around their cars to show their haute couture chosen to match their gleaming engines. When all was done, Mrs Nick Haines (White Jaguar) won the Grand Prix d'Honneur. This BARC novelty was to prove the first of a series.

The competition season concluded with the Goodwood September meeting in steady rain. At long last the BRM finally appeared. It came to the line in the hands of Reg Parnell, the most experienced driver in the country. Having had to come through the field in one of the earlier heats the feature race saw Parnell streak away to win by nearly 13 seconds at 82.5mph in twelve laps. Then the Hon. Denis Berry of Kemsley Press handed Parnell the trophy for the third successive year.

The year 1951 opened with the Council's reluctant decision not to run another financially disastrous race in Jersey where the local authorities wished to change the date to 10 May – four days before an international meeting at Goodwood. It was therefore thought prudent to rest the race for that year and reconsider the matter in 1952.

Above: Dinner dance – social occasions were just as important to some BARC members as the racing.

Above right: Group Captain Marlow and Miss J. Musgrove at the 1956 Concours D'Elegance.

Right: Another view of the 1956 Concours D'Elegance held on 16 July as part of the Eastbourne Rally.

Mike Hawthorn.

Some 100 members attended the AGM. The claim for heavy damages arising from the 1949 fatalities in Jersey had been heard in the courts and decided in favour of the club on all points. Matters moved on. Incompetent driving or inconsiderate driving in the Members' Meeting at Goodwood occupied some time – several competitors were carpeted before the stewards and duly reprimanded. The Council decided that discipline must be tightened in future. This happened with a rule to the effect that whoever spun off several times would be hauled off the course forthwith. Next came the growing demand for a long-distance race being noted and the Events Committee began to explore the possibilities in that direction. This led to the Nine Hours Race and then to the RAC Tourist Trophy eventually being held at Goodwood.

In April 179 new members joined up and in June no fewer than 383 more. This brought the total up to 4,282 with all the Centres reporting increased membership. There were three international meetings in 1951, as before. The circuit had been resurfaced during the winter and was in fine condition ready for the Easter meeting. It was the Whitsun meeting that was the best of the series. In the International 500cc Trophy Race Stirling Moss drove the new Kieft, rival to the dominant Coopers, having just arrived by air from Italy where his HWM had finished third at Monza behind Alberto Ascari and Luigi Villoresi in Ferraris. With the Kieft he won the fastest 500cc race yet run at 82.3mph and set a record lap at 84.55mph.

While Stirling Moss was beginning his meteoric climb up the ladder, the Members' Meeting on 16 June produced another new star. He was the tall, ash-blond young Mike Hawthorn driving a prewar Riley tuned by his father Leslie at their Farnham garage. Mike won the first race by a clear 10 seconds at 75.4mph and the last handicap at 77.5mph with one lap at 79.6mph. These exploits won him 13 points in the Brooklands Memorial Trophy put up by *Motor Sport* magazine and equal with T.A.D. Crook (Frazer-Nash). The issue was decided on 18 August. Using the Riley again, Hawthorn won the first race while Crook won the second. Then Hawthorn clinched the matter by finishing fourth, ahead of Crook, in the concluding handicap. In scoring a total of 18 points to Crook's 17 he held the trophy for the first year.

The echo of racing engines had scarcely died away on the season and across the quiet Sussex landscape when the duke voiced his grave concern at the speeds now being attained and suggested modifications to various sections of the circuit. There was long deliberation and study. Finally it was decided to erect a light but solid-looking wall halfway across the course at the left-hand bend between Woodcote corner and the finish line where drivers were tempted to use the grass as a short cut in the more desperate finishes. Therefore Paddock Bend or the 'chicane' was introduced to form a quick right- and left-hand S-bend. This, of course, drew a line under all existing lap records but although lap speeds dropped at first – they began to mount again.

The club stepped into 1952, its fortieth year, with a membership of 4,553 and rising. It was thought prudent to go through the formalities of adding 'Ltd' to the club title for the usual reasons and the necessary wheels were accordingly set in motion.

There were two outstanding events that summer. Mrs Mirabel Topham, the vigorous and businesslike lady who owned the Grand National course at Aintree, Liverpool, was close to removing all obstacles to her project of building a £100,000 road circuit around the site. She had visited Goodwood and, impressed by the machine-like efficiency of the race organisation, she now approached the club to offer them the exclusive rights of managing the racing at the Aintree circuit. The Council, acknowledging the implied compliment, nonetheless debated the matter with great seriousness, for such a new step would mark a turning point not only in the club's history but its very policy. It would mean entering the sphere of motor race organisation as an almost full-time occupation with all the commercial angles involved and with the certainty of requiring an increased secretariat and even the possibility of paid race officials. As might be expected, the majority view was enthusiastic from a Council that had seen the BARC grow from a bunch of cyclecar enthusiasts into the most experienced racing club in the world. It was agreed that they should pursue any and every course that led to greater prestige and influence for the club and to the greater good of motoring sport as a whole. Negotiations were opened and a new page was turned on which in three years was to be inscribed: 'Organisers of the RAC Grand Prix of Great Britain'. Something of a change from a hillclimb in South Harting.

The other important event was the staging of Britain's first racing by night. This was the first Goodwood Nine Hours for sports cars. Racing was from 3.00 p.m. until midnight, bringing a flavour of Le Mans 24 Hours to the Sussex countryside. The *News of the World* came forward with no less than £1,000 as first prize and a further £1,500 to be distributed among the less successful. The pits were illuminated and something close to the Continental atmosphere was created. There was a field of thirty cars to run in three classes and a General Category without handicap. The winners were Peter Collins and Pat Griffith at 75.4mph. The crowd, regrettably, was small.

That season too the Jersey Road Race was revived although to keep costs down it was restricted to sports cars. The winner was Ian Stewart of David Murray's Ecurie Ecosse (Jaguar) at 87.8mph, only 3mph slower than the fastest Grand Prix car in previous years. Once again, however, the race was a success but the financial return was not. Guarantors on the island were faced with repairing a gap of some £2,000 between receipts and expenditure. With the existence of circuits in England and the mounting costs of organising racing in Jersey the club at last reluctantly decided to wind up the series with this fifth and last race.

However, before this slight depression arrived, the season opened at Goodwood on Easter Monday before a very good attendance. The new chicane – Paddock Bend – was in place. A very solid-looking wall stretched halfway across the track from the outside grass verge and despite the flowers along its parapet, it looked faintly menacing to the drivers on the first practice day. Its solidity, however, was skin deep, for a big section was mounted on rollers to swing away even on a light impact with little or no resistance. On the inside verge there was erected another wall, or fence, of light wattle to demarcate the S-bend. The new corner in full view of the stands added much to the excitement of the racing for both drivers and spectators. On the infield a great ramp had to be constructed to accommodate many hundreds who congregated to 'see the fun' of which there was plenty when the 'learner drivers' were mastering the craft of motor racing with more zeal than skill. From that day a new list of lap records was started in a programme of first-class racing before a record attendance of more than 50,000.

Mike Hawthorn in a Cooper Bristol finished second to the world-famous José Froilán Gonzáles who was driving a Ferrari 'Thin Wall Special' in the Richmond Trophy and added to his stature in this his first season of serious racing when at the subsequent Whitsun meeting he ran away with the fifteen-lap Sussex Trophy and put in a lap at 87.27mph – one second slower than Gonzáles' record.

At the outset of 1953 there were no fewer than 104 race meetings on the card in Britain without counting an equal number of national race meetings. There were circuits operating at Goodwood, Boreham in Essex, Brands Hatch in Kent, Charterhall in Scotland, Silverstone, Castle Combe and in the near future at Aintree, Crystal Palace and Oulton Park. Britain had fifteen international dates logged. The BARC, however, was fully aware of the situation and the danger of saturation and the Council decided to hold only three international meetings at Goodwood. Plans about Aintree were still very much in the air when the season opened. In the meantime the Goodwood fixtures were to be the Easter Monday meeting, the Nine Hours in August and the closing meeting in September plus the usual Members' Days.

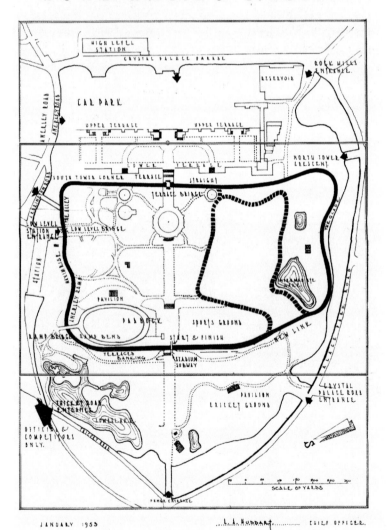

At the AGM it was agreed that the club should be officially a limited company. This meant, basically, that if ever it were necessary to wind up then members would stand to lose no more than 10s per head.

The next development to occupy the Council was the invitation from the London County Council to stage the first meeting at the Crystal Palace circuit. This was soon to be reopened and operated as another LCC attraction to the public. In mid-May, on the hottest summer day for nine years, the old Crystal Palace circuit of prewar years was reopened with a BARC meeting on London's own circuit. The famous gardens once again shook to the throaty roar of racing engines and thousands of Londoners thronged the enclosures and packed the grandstands overlooking the start area. Once again the traditional efficiency of the club was seen in action. Races started on time, competitors in the next event were marshalled at the ready and the entire affair ran like a well-oiled machine, thanks to the efforts of volunteer club members, as usual.

Opening meeting at Crystal Palace in 1953.

The *Autosport* magazine of 29 May 1953 concurred under the heading of 'Motor Racing in the Metropolis'. It went on to say:

Estimates of the crowd at last Monday's Crystal Palace race meeting – the first since August 1939 – varied from 60,000 to 100,000 but whatever the exact figure there was a terrific public attendance. From North, South, East and West London they flocked to the grounds filling every enclosure, lining the walls and terraces and every vantage point around the rebuilt, shorter, faster 1.39 mile course. From beneath sun hats, caps, eyeshades, kerchiefs or humbler head protectors such as newspapers, they watched in blazing sunshine the running of six races within three hours. And the organisers, the BARC staging the meeting on behalf of London County Council, did it all with the slickness characterising the old Road Racing Club of pre-War Palace days.

Above: A healthy attendance at Crystal Palace in 1953.

Right: A variety of headgear at Crystal Palace!

The feature race was the Coronation Trophy for Formula 2 (2-litre) cars run in two heats and a final in which Tim Rolt (Connaught), driving for patron Rob Walker, won the first and Peter Whitehead (Cooper with Alta engine) the second. Rolt won the final bagging the record lap at 72.73mph on the way. Stirling Moss won the 500cc race and this was becoming a habit with him. Looking back on those days he said:

> I didn't take part in any serious races there but it was great to have a track in the middle of town. There were trees next to the circuit but in those days we accepted the dangers. It was a tricky track in places and only about a mile around as I recall. It was great to have a London track. So convenient.

From every point of view that first meeting was a success. Some 43,000 people paid £10,500 which would have recouped the LCC's outlay.

Not so happy was the result of the second Nine Hours Race at Goodwood on 22 August, apart from the opening of the Brooklands Memorial Garden in the Paddock, a ceremony presided over by the Duke of Richmond and Gordon. This little walled plot included a slab of the old concrete banking presented by Sammy Davis. About thirty drivers who had raced on the 'Great Concrete Saucer' were among the crowd as the duke unveiled the memorial plaque. Meanwhile it could not be said that the race was an organisers' success. The gate was even smaller than before and the entry was not very good and lacked foreign competition on account of the demand for too much starting money. Without sponsorship from Fleet Street there was very little pre-race publicity in the national press and all these facets contributed to a loss.

At the final international meeting on 26 September the great Juan Fangio was no match for Mike Hawthorn now at the wheel of the 4.5-litre 'Thin Wall Special' Ferrari. The main race, the fifteen-lap Goodwood

Above: Tim Rolt waves the Coronation Trophy.

Left: Mike Hawthorn in the 'Thin Wall Special'.

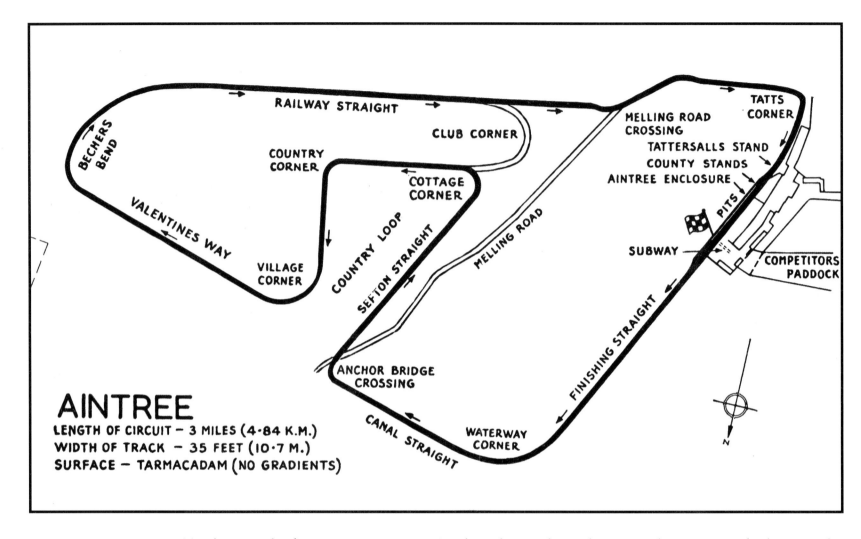

AINTREE
LENGTH OF CIRCUIT – 3 MILES (4·84 K.M.)
WIDTH OF TRACK – 35 FEET (10·7 M.)
SURFACE – TARMACADAM (NO GRADIENTS)

Trophy, saw the fastest race yet run at Goodwood. Hawthorn shot away drawing even further into the distance despite all of Fangio's efforts which ended when he lost fourth gear. The average was 92.7mph, the new lap record 94.53mph.

The club's traditional Continental Rally was revived after an interval of fifteen years. The route of some 1,500 miles went through the Black Forest into the Tyrol and back through Switzerland. It began with a party at the Burlington Hotel in Folkestone and ended with a happy gathering in a nightclub.

That winter's annual dinner and dance filled the Grosvenor House Great Room with a record guest list of 900. At the same time work was going ahead fast on Mrs Topham's Aintree circuit with all problems having been solved at last. The Council were already drawing up plans to open the course with a revival of the classic 200 Miles Race.

Only formal business occupied the 1954 AGM in March when the membership was climbing past 7,000 and the funds stood at £16,000. The racing season that year underlined the fears that too many races and too many circuits were already leading to a fall in public interest. Goodwood was counting 25,000 to 30,000 at the big meetings but this was about 10,000 short of the required target. Demands for start money were going up at a time when spectators wanted to see the great stars and the leading foreign teams in dramatic races. Racing for 500cc cars was already losing its appeal because of its inevitable sameness. As the season drew to a close the President announced that with costs up and attendances down then a financial sponsor from outside was again essential.

The major and historic event of the year was the opening of the Aintree circuit with an international meeting on 29 May. Dismal rain swept the 3-mile circuit all morning and well into the afternoon. It stopped only for the final of the 200 Miles Race run in two heats and the decider. The depressing weather produced a somewhat depressed attendance of 25,000.

The opening event was a ten-lap sportscar race with a Le Mans-style start which entailed the drivers running as hard as they could across the track to their waiting cars – parked with their noses pointing down the course. In pouring rain the drivers took off with Jimmy Stewart (older brother of Jackie) in a Jaguar XK 120C of the Ecurie Ecosse in the lead, hotly pursued by Duncan Hamilton in a similar model. With three laps to go Hamilton splashed past in a trailing cloud of spume and Texan Carroll Shelby followed with his DB 3S Aston Martin, beating Stewart into third place. Hamilton won at 79.37mph by 8 seconds. For reasons that seemed good at the time, the racing was conducted in an anti-clockwise direction – probably to give the spectators in a long line of grandstands and terraces a view of the cars passing at high speed. This was changed for subsequent meetings and the fact that the cars had to accelerate out of a tight curve into the straight did nothing to reduce the drama.

The '200' was a free formula race in two heats of seventeen laps (51 miles) and a final of thirty-four laps (102 miles). Heat one fell to Reg Parnell (Ferrari) at 76.97mph with the famous 'Thin Wall Special' driven by Peter Collins 12 seconds behind. Ron Flockhart (BRM) won heat two at 76.9mph only 3 seconds in front of Roy Salvadori's Maserati. In the final Stirling Moss won the first of his series of victories at Aintree driving a Grand Prix 2.5-litre Maserati at 77.7mph. He was a good half-minute ahead of Parnell's Ferrari. It was indeed Moss's day. He won the ten-lap 500cc race in the Beart-Cooper and was third in his heat for the '200'. Five races were run off with BARC precision after which the crowds dispersed, the car parks emptied quickly and everyone was on their way home with an ease uncommon at most circuits.

The meeting was experimental and comments conflicted. Drivers thought the circuit too slow on account of so many corners, especially the re-entrant triangle to Cottage Corner and back where the course dived away from the outer perimeter into the infield to bring the lap up to 3 miles. Indeed Moss stated that there was as much gear-changing as at Monte Carlo, making this a 'drivers' circuit' if ever there was one.

The Events Committee recommended that the races should be run in the normal international fashion – clockwise. Racing the other way around when most corners were left-handers meant that the curves tightened up instead of opening out, therefore reducing the lap speeds and increasing the hazards. Also, the pits could not be operated with the usual ease.

In the autumn of that year, when the club decided to expand its racing activities whenever an opportunity offered and thereby founded its present fortunes and prestige, the second historic decision was made. The Royal Automobile Club Grand Prix of Great Britain, a Grande Epreuve ranking for the World Championship, had been delegated for several years to the British Racing Drivers Club at Silverstone. It was supported by the *Daily Express* and not financed by the RAC, since they ran their own races there from 1948 to 1951. The Competitions Committee now decided that it was right and proper to offer the Grand Prix to the BARC on the Aintree circuit for 1955 and thereafter in alternate years to the club and the BRDC. The Council considered the matter with all its implications and accepted the offer. The *Daily Telegraph* directors at once promised all their support for this important event and the club: this was a proper occasion to guarantee a sum of £2,000 from the Motor Sports Fund. Another great step had been taken.

With the membership now topping 8,000, plus the increased number of events being organised, the club acquired a new suite of offices at 10 South Street, adjoining the main offices at 55 Park Lane for the transaction of members' business, such as the sale of tickets, badges and the like. During that season the club ran seven major public meetings. There were three at Goodwood, two at Aintree and two at Crystal Palace. Also three Members' Meetings took place at Goodwood, a Members' Sprint at Aintree and the ever-popular Eastbourne Rally and Concours. That all this activity was carried through with a machine-like efficiency was a tribute to the organisational abilities of the General Secretary, his assistants and the work of the army of volunteer officials who did their duty so gladly and well in the field. Even the running of two international meetings within seven days did not strain the machine.

ONWARD AND UPWARD

The year 1955 marked the first time the club was authorised – on invitation – to organise the Grand Prix of Great Britain on behalf of the Royal Automobile Racing Club. The final cachet.

This was also the black year, standing out in motor racing history as the year in which a Mercedes practically exploded among a packed enclosure at Le Mans, killing more than eighty spectators on the spot and injuring at least a hundred others. The driver, Pierre Levegh, was killed instantly. Immediately the French Government banned road racing, the Swiss cancelled their Grand Prix, the Germans followed suit, and so did the Spaniards. A wave of anxiety almost amounting to panic swept across the world, well fanned by newspapers of all countries which printed large horror pictures of the carnage.

So it can be imagined that there was anxiety of a new kind added to the worries of the BARC race organisation as 16 July (the date of the British Grand Prix) drew near. The Mercedes-Benz factory sent a delegation to inspect Aintree. There was virtually no possibility of the kind of collision that had occurred at Le Mans and the Germans came, saw and declared it one of the safest circuits in Europe.

The race was not a thrilling spectacle as a competition, but the sight of four silver Mercedes driven one behind the other by Stirling Moss, Juan Fangio, Karl Kling and Piero Tarliffi – who finished in that order – held the crowds throughout. Moss and Fangio streaked to the line side by side, fighting it out to the last, for there were no team instructions. Moss won by half a length, a fifth of a second ahead. He averaged 86.5mph and broke the lap record at 89.7mph. The rest of the field was out of sight, a lap behind. This was his first victory in a Grands Epreuve. These days Sir Stirling has a clear perspective on the Aintree circuit:

The track was more difficult than many would appreciate. It was hard on brakes. You would get up to a high speed then brake hard to go off at a right angle. The centre was shaped like a clover. We had to cross over parts of the horseracing circuit but that was no inconvenience. It was also an excellent setting with the grandstands of the race circuit. It was quite a demanding track but I had a good record there.

Left: Fangio leads Moss, 1955.

Below: Moss pips Fangio, 1955.

A month later the Nine Hours was run again at Goodwood with thirty-five starters including Mike Hawthorn (Ferrari) who beat the lap record for sportscars during practice. Hawthorn appeared for the first time at Crystal Palace on 30 July, flying back from the Continent just in time to take the start in the International Trophy. He won a heat and won the final after a desperate struggle with Harry Schell's Vanwall.

It was in July of that year that the club introduced its Junior Membership scheme to attract the interest of young enthusiasts in the families of full members. For an entry fee of 5s and an annual fee of half a guinea the Juniors, between fourteen and eighteen, received a lapel badge or brooch, a card of admission to Members' Meetings, guest vouchers for their friends, a copy of the *Gazette* and admission to full membership on their eighteenth birthday without payment of an entry fee.

The Centres were equally busy with their sporting and social programmes. The South-Western Centre ran the tenth of their hillclimbs at Brunton in Wiltshire. The other Centres ran rallies, gymkhanas and the like with the utmost enthusiasm and efficiency as well as good entries.

At the annual dinner and dance of 1955 the achievements of Stirling Moss in the few years that he had been at the wheel were recognised in a signal manner with the presentation by the President of the first BARC Gold Medal. The Council decided on this tribute after Stirling had followed his triumph in the Mille Miglia by winning the British Grand Prix. For full measure he also won the Tourist Trophy and the Targa Florio, all with Mercedes.

The thousand members and friends were no less vociferous at the presentation of a gold watch to John Morgan, the General Secretary, who had notched up thirty years of service to the club. That year alone he had masterminded eleven race meetings, six open to the public, in addition to the normal and ever-increasing secretarial work.

At the October conference of the International Automobile Federation a drastic attempt was made to abbreviate the cluttered calendar after being prodded by the RAC delegate for at least four years. The solution was not exactly as had been hoped, for it hit the British clubs hard. It gave Britain five international dates among fourteen circuits. What it meant as far as the BARC was concerned was that the club had only two international fixtures in 1956. The dates for that year involved twenty meetings.

In July the club introduced a new racing rule, brought about by the numerous and unnecessary spinning-top performances that too many drivers were continually performing. The drivers possibly knew that with the wide grass verges in place, such errors were not dangerous in themselves. These gyrations, however, often resulted in the car behind colliding with the spinner or in forcing the driver to swerve off the course to avoid the shunt. It was therefore laid down that any driver who spun off (or on) the circuit through his own fault

Above left: Mike Hawthorn's victory sip.

Above: The Duke of Richmond and John Morgan.

Stirling Moss prepares for the 1957 Grand Prix.

would be automatically excluded from the race. The observers posted around the course were to be judges of fact in these cases and therefore there could be no protest against their findings.

September was a sad month with the death, at sixty-eight, of Professor A.M. Low, a founder member and an indefatigable councillor. That autumn the Suez Crisis plunged Britain into a petrol crisis and once more coupons were in use. For how long, no one knew. Now, once again, the future of motorsport looked uncertain but promoters decided to carry on as best they could.

Early in 1957 the BARC, together with other clubs, slashed their fixture list. This left only the Grand Prix at Aintree in July and the major public meetings at Goodwood. Then the government acknowledged the importance of motor racing by the special grant of petrol coupons to promoting clubs so that racing car transporters and officials in their own cars were able to get to the few meetings that could be held.

The Grand Prix of Europe was run at Aintree on 20 July and was one of the finest races yet seen in Britain. The practice was full of excitement with Moss beating his own lap record in his Vanwall. Then Tony Brooks

Above: Moss takes over Brooks' Vanwall, 1957.

Above right: Moss takes the chequered flag, 1957.

(Vanwall) and Jean Behra (Maserati) equalled it, so that the three took the front row. Moss jumped into the lead but had two quick pitstops owing to fuel starvation. Then he took over from Brooks. All this time Behra held the lead from Hawthorn with Moss closing the interval lap by lap. Just as the thrilled spectators were calculating that Moss might yet catch Behra, but only just before the end, the Maserati's clutch flew to pieces and a sharp sliver of metal punctured Hawthorn's rear wheel as he tore through the debris trailed behind Behra. Moss was about to lap Lewis-Evans again when the flag went up so the two British drivers finished together first and seventh with Musso's Ferrari in second place, 26 seconds behind. Moss bumped the lap record up to 90.6mph and averaged 86.8mph. It was not realised then but that day saw the beginning of the decline of both Maserati and Ferrari and the rise of British cars to pre-eminence.

In mid-August once again new ground was broken with a Members' Meeting at the new Mallory Park circuit near Leicester – 1.35 miles of road in pleasant parkland and for the first time a 500cc racing car event was included with the sportscar races.

The final Goodwood meeting, the national event on 28 September, provided a day of lap records, excellent racing and the smallest crowd ever known in spite of it being a glorious summer day. This once more underlined the effect of too many races on too many circuits.

However, down at Goodwood the winter was busy. A small army of men was at work transforming the appearance of the circuit. A subway for spectators on foot was driven under Lavant Straight to open up a new enclosure on the inside of the course. Another, wide enough for vehicles and high enough for transporters and lorries, was built under the finishing straight communicating with the Paddock and the infield car parks beyond. The Paddock itself was redesigned with lines of roofed stalls fenced off from the public who could still watch the mechanics at work. Members could now motor to distant parts of the circuit, park up and use their cars as grandstands. Two landing strips were cleared for light aircraft.

There was by now hardly any room left for more feathers in the BARC cap, but another was added in 1958 when the RAC invited the club to organise the Tourist Trophy for them at Goodwood. Since the black year of 1955 this historic race, founded on the Isle of Man in 1905, had been abandoned as the circuit at Dundrod was judged to be too narrow for the speeds of the fastest sportscars racing in among the small fry. Although it was admitted that the Goodwood circuit was by no means ideal for such a race (which belonged by its very nature and long tradition on a true road circuit), the BARC readily agreed to undertake the enterprise. In doing so they kept the race on the international calendar where it had ranked as a World Championship event. The date, 13 September, was therefore firmly booked.

Once again in 1958 the FIA allowed the calendar to fix too many of the same kind of races at too close intervals. The Events Committee were gravely concerned. The Easter Meeting had always been the first international reunion of the leading teams after the winter modifications where their paces could be tried before the first European race in the world series at Monte Carlo in mid-May. Now the available cars would be split between Goodwood and the Pau Grand Prix on the same day, 7 April, for a start. After that there would be very little spare time for preparing the machines for the races one after another which could have the effect of producing cars out of tune and a high percentage of retirements. The club's plan was to run a 100-mile Grand Prix 'trial' at Goodwood followed two weeks later by a full-distance 200-mile race – this being the regulation distance for a Formula 1 Grand Prix. All this now seemed imperilled together with the finance involved, for the public could now pick and choose the circuit where they spent their money and might stay away in large numbers unless the top line drivers and cars were present.

Moss and Brooks share the laurels in 1957.

*The start of the 1958
Aintree 200.*

The eventual club programme added up to fourteen race meetings to keep the machinery of organisation ticking over and, of course, at the big meetings there were not merely the Grand Prix type of event but supporting races as well.

The other side of club life was by no means being neglected. Among the social fixtures were the Eastbourne Rally and Concours, the annual dinner in November and a Christmas Party. In June there was a trip down the Thames and back. Nor were the devotees of trials and rally driving left out, for BARC members had a choice of twenty-seven such events to which they were invited by other clubs. By now the club's branch in the South-East had been raised in status to a Centre and was joined by a new group based in Leicester. The Centres, going from strength to strength, were running over forty events of all kinds as well as social functions, film shows and lectures.

Plans were being drawn up for the RAC Tourist Trophy on 13 September. Once again the *News of the World* assisted the BARC with prize money of £2,000. It was decided that the race should be of 4 hours'

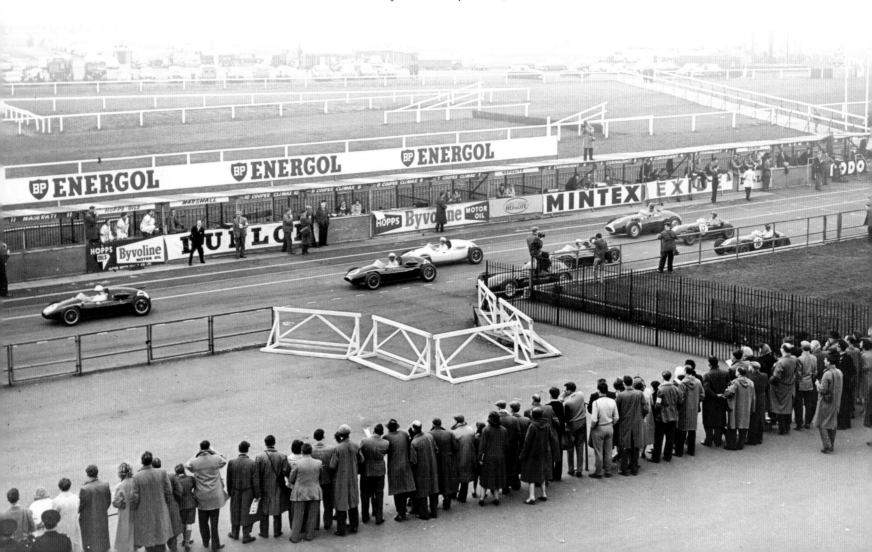

duration from 2.00 p.m., thus counting for half-marks in the Manufacturers' Championship. The full regulation 6-hour stint was deemed too hard on the stamina of cars and drivers on the short and winding Goodwood course and a finish of 6.00 p.m. was thought to please the public who had distances to travel home afterwards.

So came the long-awaited Tourist Trophy experiment in mid-September. A disappointment, by the unpredictable Enzo Ferrari, was the absence of his cars in spite of his promise to send them over. As such there was no serious opposition to the team of 3-litre Aston Martins. Belgian and Swiss entries failed to appear and only one Ecurie Ecosse Jaguar could be prepared in time. The contest became a procession of three Aston Martins followed at a respectful distance by a German Porsche, followed by two Jaguars. At the end, team manager Reg Parnell formed his cars up in line astern. They crossed the line at intervals of one length, less than one second covering the three. The experiment was a success and the crowd enjoyed the spectacle. Only eight of the twenty-nine starters retired. The Tourist Trophy was on its own again and returned to Goodwood each year until the circuit closed.

That winter, when the sound of racing cars was stilled, there was celebration in the dignified salons of the RAC in Pall Mall. The happy occasion was the presentation of the FIA plaque to World Champion Mike Hawthorn and champion manufacturers Tony Vandervell (Formula 1, Vanwall) and Charles Cooper (Formula 2, Cooper).

At the annual dinner of 1958 Mike Hawthorn was presented with the BARC Gold Medal in tribute to his World Championship on the eve of his retirement from active racing. Sadly, in January 1959 he was killed in his private car on a road near Guildford in Surrey.

Also in 1959, the General Secretary recounted the membership and reported to the Council that it had climbed to over 14,000 and was showing no sign of abating its increase. It was a year of expansion again. Seventeen race meetings were staged including both the RAC classics – the Grand Prix at Aintree and the Tourist Trophy at Goodwood. New groups were being established in Worcester, Leatherhead and Tredegar.

A new club was set up more remotely, in Toronto, Canada, as its first President, John Bowles, recalls:

Before emigrating to Canada in 1957 I had been a BARC member in the UK. The club had an active Centre in South-West England and I came from Devon. It put on rally and slalom events in which me and my supercharged Ford-engined Dellow did well and I enjoyed the club's membership. I also discovered that the club had a few members in Toronto. My previous association with BARC led me to contact John Morgan – then parent Secretary – to see if the club Council would entertain the formation of an Ontario Centre. After all, the club had Centres throughout the UK, there were already some members in Toronto, so why not?

The proposal generated considerable back and forth discussions as I recall but eventually the Council approved the creation of what is still the only BARC Centre outside the UK. For the record the exact formation date was 27 October 1959.

With the parent club's approval came some conditions. These included regular reporting of the new Centre's progress, a minimum of twenty-five first members and from our number a Chairman or President to be elected. That turned out to be me! It didn't take too long to increase membership, create committees and start arranging meetings and small events. Organising ice and circuit races came later.

BARC Ontario Centre's ice racing.

I also thought that the club should have a patron, a figurehead, a person of prominence. At that time Stirling Moss was the most renowned racing driver in the world. So it was to him I addressed a letter of invitation to not only be the club's patron but for good measure to donate a perpetual trophy as well. Again, why not? If you don't ask, you don't get. Well, he accepted and donated a trophy.

Following the success of an experimental race the previous Whitsun, the Events Committee introduced yet another new kind of race at the Members' Meetings in 1958 known as the 'Marque Race' open to cars specified by the organisers and selected because their type and performance were much the same. Even certain models of a given make, known to be faster, were excluded in the interests of equality. So successful was this event that it continued for many seasons.

Meanwhile, the number of committees had now been pared down to four – Events, Finance and General Purposes and Membership Elections and Development. It was a streamlining exercise that coped with all business more quickly.

Also, besides the Members' Meetings at Goodwood, Aintree and Mallory Park there was, for the first time, a similar event at Oulton Park in Cheshire.

The Easter Monday Goodwood meeting was the first major gathering and held in uncertain weather. Earlier, while the track was dry, a new record went up in the 1,100cc sportscar race when Peter Ashdown took his Lola around at an oustanding 90.38mph. Stirling Moss (Cooper) won the Formula 1 100-mile race on a streaming circuit at 90.3mph. Jack Brabham (Cooper) was 17 seconds behind. Next day Moss tried a BRM in private session and for the first time Goodwood was lapped at over 100mph.

The British Grand Prix at Aintree on 18 July was run in perfect weather. On his way to his first World Championship, the Australian Jack Brabham, driving one of the two Coopers entered by the factory, led the 225-mile race from start to finish pursued by Stirling Moss. Bruce McLaren (Cooper) equalled Stirling Moss' record lap at 92.31mph and the two cars – Moss in a private BRM – shot across the finish line 22 seconds behind Brabham and one-fifth of a second apart!

The winter months were enlivened with less formal parties and the Midnight Matinée of films at the Curzon Cinema in Mayfair had to be repeated on several nights. There was much speculation on the prospects for 1960 – the last year of the 2.5-litre formula that had lasted since 1954 and had seen such dynamic changes. What the club decided without demur was to continue and expand the air trips to major

Continental races. These flights had been widely used by drivers and their entourages as well as by spectators and from all accounts the journeys were whiled away in considerable festivity.

The Events Committee, their finger on the pulse of development, announced that in 1960 there would be events for the very vigorous new Formula Junior which had already attained enthusiastic support in this country and virtually replaced 500cc racing, now quite out of favour. Like that form of racing in the early post-war years the Juniors were meant to be a 'poor man's' section of the sport for the cars were relatively inexpensive and could even be home-built with every chance of success. In simple terms they were single-seater racing cars with standard production 1,100cc or 1,000cc engines of the types using pushrods instead of overhead camshafts with standard brakes and gearboxes but in any kind of chassis to choice. Dozens of these cars had been built and raced with quite astonishing success. In addition to Cooper, Lotus, Lola and Elva (who were already familiar in sportscar racing and now in the Junior market), there were at least a score more, almost all propelled by the Ford 997cc unit or the BMC 994cc engine. There were similar

Jack Brabham takes the flag in 1959.

cars in Italy, Germany, France and the idea was spreading to America and Canada. The BARC decided to encourage it at every possible meeting.

Ferrari sent a team to the Tourist Trophy at Goodwood on 5 September, for they were battling Aston Martin for the Sports Car Championship that year and Porsche were there too for the same reason. Ferrari had 18 points, Aston Martin 16 and Porsche 15. The event was therefore the decider and was to be run for the full six hours to qualify for the full number of championship points. The cars were again limited to at most 3-litre capacity in accordance with FIA law.

From third place Stirling Moss (Aston Martin) drove into the lead to win by 3 miles at 89.41mph. The Porsche (von Trips and Bonnier) was second with Brooks and Gendebien (Ferrari) third. So Moss snatched victory from defeat and handed the championship to Mr David Brown – the first time the title had come to Britain. Once again, however, the crowd was disappointingly small. It proved for the fifth time that long-distance sportscar races had little grip on any but the true believers.

OFFICIAL PROGRAMME 1s.

CRYSTAL PALACE

national (open) race meeting
ORGANISED BY BRITISH AUTOMOBILE RACING CLUB

Whit Monday 6 June 1960

LONDON COUNTY COUNCIL

The Autocar

There had to be two Gold Medals that year for presentation at the annual dinner. One to Mr David Brown, the first British winner of the World Championship of Sports Car Manufacturers and again to John Cooper – not only had he won the equivalent title in Formula 1 but in Formula 2 as well and that for the second year.

At the AGM in March the President warmly congratulated the Hon General Treasurer, Frank Bale, who was confirmed in that duty for the forty-second year.

The basic plan for 1960 was to turn the Aintree 200 (30 April) into a Formula 2 race, making this the British event in the championship series. Also to run a 100km (62-mile) race at Oulton Park where the meeting would be national on 2 April and the 100-mile 'Grand Prix Trial' as the main event in the International Goodwood Meeting on Easter Monday 18 April.

The National event at Oulton Park, the club's first big meeting at that Cheshire circuit, was another pronounced success that started the BARC off on its busy year's programme with confidence. Five races were run off, of which Lotus cars won all but the Marque Race for which they were not eligible. The twenty-five-lap Trophy race (Formula 2) was won by a driver who was rapidly emerging into the limelight – Innes Ireland – with the new rear-engined model. There was also another newcomer all set to make a mark – John Surtees, champion of champions in the motorcycle world.

Jim Clark (Lotus) won the Junior ten-lap race. His average of 85.98mph may be compared with that of Ireland at 91.1mph. Clark's best lap at 87.5mph was only 5.6 seconds slower than Ireland's – about 2 seconds per mile.

The good start at Oulton Park was maintained at Goodwood a fortnight later on a bright spring day before a record crowd. Although a poor crowd

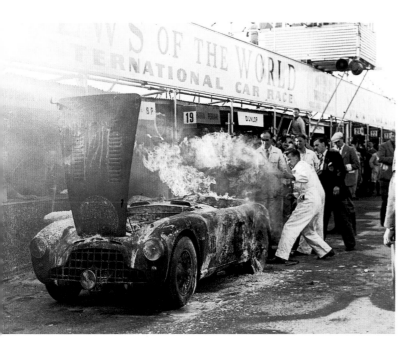

such as those at the Nine Hours and Tourist Trophy races had a depressing effect on the revenue, this did not directly affect the BARC finances. The club staged and managed the racing for an agreed sum. It was, for instance, Goodwood Road Racing Co. Ltd (of which the club President was the head) that provided the course and its installations then footed the bill. Naturally a deficit too great or too often would make the financing of racing open to review. However, if the swings failed, then the roundabouts usually made up.

There was a somewhat startling new award on offer that day – the Goodwood Ton – for the first drivers to dash around the circuit in a race at 100mph. This underlined the progress in the design of engines, chassis and especially tyres over the previous three or four years. At the end three young men queued for their 'Tons': Stirling Moss (Cooper), Innes Ireland (Lotus) and Graham Hill (rear-engined BRM).

Goodwood acquired another link with the Brooklands tradition when Tommy Wisdom, the journalist and racing driver of thirty years' standing, presented the club with the actual gates that used to open the Paddock onto the track, these together with a lamp standard from the same site. The gates were to perform their old function, opening from the Goodwood Paddock onto the marshalling area which led to the circuit, while the lamp stood in the little garden surrounding the pavilion of the Guild of Motoring Writers. On the gates was a plate reading: 'Every driver who raced at Brooklands from its opening in 1907 to the close in 1939 passed through these gates from the Paddock to the track. Presented to the BARC by Tommy Wisdom.'

The experiment of running the Tourist Trophy for Grand Touring Cars only on 20 August was clearly a success. The racing was quite as thrilling as before when the 3-litre sportscars were competing, but the

Above left: An Aston Martin on fire in the pits at Goodwood.

Above: John Cooper and Sir David Brown.

Bale, Morgan and Follett.

crowd was even smaller although there was a curtain-raiser in the form of the first BARC Formula Junior Championship with two heats and a final, so giving the crowd three more races. This classic race and the forty-third Members' Meeting at Goodwood a few weeks later brought the competition season to its close and with it the Grand Prix formula that had lasted seven years, the longest in the history of Grand Prix racing since 1906.

The BARC had just over 16,000 members – a growth of almost fifteen times its numbers when motorsport began after the war and an increase unprecedented in club life. The club sailed into 1961 with nineteen race meetings in the diary. Four international, four national and the remainder were for members clamouring for events.

THE BEGINNING OF THE END

When the 1,500cc Formula 1 was first proposed, British motorsport opposed the move and continued to oppose it. This led to the two British engine-builders, Coventry Climax and BRM, being behind with new engines. It also led to Britain staging a rival series, the Inter-Continental Formula, which was for cars up to 3 litres. In effect it was a series for surviving Formula 1 cars.

At the 1961 Goodwood Easter meeting, the Lavant Cup was run to the Inter-Continental Formula. There was a field of only nine but it included Brooks, Gurney, Graham Hill, McLaren, Moss, Salvadori and Surtees. Moss (Cooper) came from behind to overtake McLaren (Cooper) on the last lap of fifteen to win by 0.6 seconds. Hill (BRM) was third some 20 seconds behind. However, the Inter-Continental Series fizzled out after just five races.

The feature Formula 1 race, the Glover Trophy, saw John Surtees win in a private Lotus 18. John's car racing was fitted in with his winning the Motorcycle World Championship for MV Augusta. As John explains:

The first time that I tried out in a race car was at Goodwood. It was the winter of 1958 and it was an Aston Martin DB R1 which Reg Parnell brought down. The next day Tony Vandervell gave me a Vanwall to try. Eventually my first competitive race was at Goodwood in a GT in a Formula Junior event. I had never ridden Goodwood as a motorcyclist whereas I had ridden Aintree as a motorcyclist previously. Goodwood is fairly unique and hasn't changed. It had quick corners and in a non-aerodynamic era this brought out the difference in drivers. The circuit allowed you to get a rhythm and it was a bit of a teaser, especially at Fordwater. I have good memories of racing at Goodwood.

Before the 1961 Tourist Trophy race the organisers ordered a special cake with seven candles on it. Stirling Moss was on the entry list and few doubted that he would win his seventh TT. Mike Parkes who, like Moss, was in a Ferrari 250 GT SWB, went into the lead followed by Clark and Salvadori in Aston Martin

The start of the 1961 Grand Prix at Aintree.

Zagotas. Then came Moss. Stirling was second by the end of the first lap and took the lead from Parkes after seventeen laps. He disappeared into the distance and duly received his cake in the shape of a number seven. He had won the Tourist Trophy for the seventh time but would not return since he would crash at Goodwood the following April.

1961 was also a busy year for Aintree which once again hosted the British Grand Prix in addition to the International 200. Aintree's first event, the International 200 meeting, took place on 22 April. As was the normal practice, the programme for the day included four races and attracted a fine entry. Just before the main race of the day there was a tremendous downpour. Fortunately, Dunlop had produced a new rain tyre which most of the teams chose to use. By the end of the first lap Jack Brabham led from Jim Clark, Bruce McLaren, Graham Hill and John Surtees. Stirling Moss was in eighth place with Innes Ireland and Roy Salvadori behind him. The race ended with Brabham finishing clear of his team-mate McLaren by about 12 seconds. Despite the atrocious conditions the winner's average speed was 78.06mph and the fastest lap was set by McLaren at exactly 80mph. Both Cooper drivers had given a superb demonstration of high-speed wet-weather driving.

In the third weekend of July the teams travelled to Aintree for the fourteenth RAC British Grand Prix. Again the rain was very heavy well before the 2.30 p.m. start time. The new Dunlop rain tyre was back in demand and all but one driver elected to use a visor. Off the grid the thirty cars disappeared towards Waterway Corner in a huge cloud of spray.

Two red cars were visible leading the pack and at Anchor Crossing – it was Phil Hill in front of his Ferrari team-mate Wolfgang von Trips. The conditions were dreadful with the track flooded in places. On lap six Henry Taylor crashed in his Lotus at Melling Crossing and was taken to hospital after being cut free from the wreckage. Fortunately, his injuries did not prove to be serious. Leader Phil Hill slowed down as a result of Taylor's accident and this allowed von Trips to take the lead, which he was to hold to the finish as part of a Ferrai 1-2-3 also featuring Richie Ginther. In winning the British Grand Prix Wolfgang von Trips had driven a race average of 83.91mph for the seventy-five laps. He took the lead in the World Championship but was killed later in the season at the Italian Grand Prix at Monza. His team-partner Phil Hill went on to take the title.

Wolfgang von Trips at Aintree in 1961.

The final BARC meeting of 1961 came at Crystal Palace on 2 September. The main event was the September Trophy for Formula Junior Cars. Heat one went to Dennis Taylor in his privately-entered Lola-Ford and namesake Trevor Taylor won the second heat in the works Lotus-Ford. The twenty-five-lap final saw the two Taylors vying for the lead. The Lola led for eight laps before the Lotus took over and went on to win by 3.5 seconds.

Racing fans were able to witness that more work was being completed on the building of the National Sports Centre, which had been announced by Sir Isaac Howard, leader of the LCC, in the summer of 1960 as a facility to offer 'Sport For All'. Administration of the scheme was entrusted to the Central Council for Physical Recreation and in the *Motor Cycle* a correspondent wrote of his anxiety that this body might not look on the sport in a favourable light: 'The area is big enough for both a race and an Athletics crowd but conflict could arise.' Urging the ACU and RAC to press the claims of the Palace as a motorsports venue,

Jim Clark and Colin Chapman at the Aintree 200 in 1962.

he warned, 'A road racing circuit in the heart of London is an asset we certainly cannot afford to lose.' This was to prove prophetic but Crystal Palace would survive the decade unlike certain other circuits.

Controversy had raged when during the second half of 1961 the RAC announced that the 1962 British Grand Prix would be held at Aintree rather than Silverstone as expected. The reason given by the RAC was that the BARC would be celebrating its Golden Jubilee in 1962 and it was therefore appropriate for the club to stage the Grand Prix. The BARC's rival organisation, the British Racing Drivers' Club (BRDC) was stunned and a storm of protest took place.

Nevertheless, the RAC stood by its decision and the British Grand Prix was scheduled to take place at Aintree on 21 July 1962. It can be safely assumed that few who took part in the heated arguments regarding the RAC's decision were aware at the time that this would be the last Grand Prix staged at the Liverpool venue.

Despite the British drivers having had a thin time of it in 1961, matters seemed to be better for British teams by the Easter 1962 meeting at Goodwood. V8 engines from BRM and Coventry Climax had begun to appear with selected teams. Goodwood therefore ran two Formula 1 races: the Lavant Cup for four-cylinder cars and the Glover Trophy for all-comers. The Lavant Cup attracted mainly privateers and was won by Bruce McLaren in a works Cooper. The Glover Trophy was the race which ended Stirling Moss's glittering career, for while Graham Hill went on to win in his BRM, Stirling Moss crashed at St Mary's and ended the day comatose in intensive care. Graham Hill subsequently took the 1962 World Championship with Jim Clark second. As British motor racing grew in stature, so the races at Goodwood grew in quality.

Meanwhile, the first Aintree event of the year, the International 200 meeting, took place on 28 April. The race was the first occasion in 1962 when all the leading teams were to meet in competition. There was great interest in the prospect of the top British teams competing against Ferraris now that the home teams had V8 power. Sadly, number seven for the fifty-lap Formula 1 200 was shown as withdrawn. That was Stirling Moss's favourite racing number and had been allocated to him prior to his serious accident at Goodwood.

The event stared at 3.30 p.m. At the drop of the flag Ginther made a superb start from the second row of the grid and led the field in his BRM. Ginther's team-mate Graham Hill took second place and at the end of the first lap the order behind the two BRM's was Clark, McLaren, Phil Hill and Ireland. By lap twenty-five Clark was leading by 34 seconds at an average speed of 94.48mph – faster than the previous outright lap record! Graham Hill was now in second pace as Ginther had retired with gearbox problems. Then came Surtees, Phil Hill and McLaren. How times had changed since 1961 when the Ferraris were so dominant.

Jim Clark finished the race with a winning margin of 1 minute 30 seconds with McLaren in second place and Phil Hill third. Clark's average speed was 92.65mph and he set the fastest lap in 1 minute 54.0 seconds with a speed of 94.74mph, which was both a new Formula 1 and outright lap record. So ended the record-breaking 1962 Aintree 200 meeting in which Lotus cars won each of the three races they entered.

A late Easter date meant that 11 June was the next Bank Holiday for the BARC to promote a national meeting with Formula 1 cars topping the bill at Crystal Palace. Roy Salvadori was favourite to win in his Bowmaker Racing Lola-Climax V8, but despite starting from pole position he was unable to compete with a brilliant Innes Ireland who came from the back of the grid in his UDT-Laystall Lotus-BRM V8 and

Jim Clark's Lotus at the Aintree 200 in April 1962.

Jim Clark at the 1962
Grand Prix at Aintree.

chopped nearly 2.5 seconds off the lap record of Salvadori and Henry Taylor to leave it at 57.2 seconds and 87.46mph. Salvadori had to settle for second place while Bruce McLaren brought the works Cooper-Climax home third.

That year the Tourist Trophy race at Goodwood was reduced to 100 laps, roughly 2 hours. Jim Clark (Aston Martin) got the best start but was soon passed by the GTOs of Ireland, Surtees and Graham Hill. On the second lap Surtees moved into the lead. On lap sixty-two Surtees came up to lap Clark for the second time. Jim lost it at Madgwick's and rammed John. Innes Ireland inherited the lead and held it eventually from Graham Hill and Mike Parkes by 3.4 seconds.

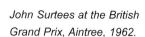

John Surtees at the British
Grand Prix, Aintree, 1962.

The British Grand Prix was round five of the World Championship. All the teams had full entries at Aintree on 21 July with the sole exception of Ferrari, which had one car for Phil Hill. Jim Clark stamped his authority on the event from the outset. He was over half a second faster in practice than Surtees with Ireland third fastest and McLaren fourth. In contrast to the previous year's race, the weather was dry and sunny when the race started at 2.30 p.m. Clark immediately took the lead and drove off into the distance, leaving the rest of the field to fight among themselves. At lap thirty the order was Clark, Surtees, McLaren, Graham Hill, Brabham and Gurney. The only change in this order came when Tony Maggs passed Gurney to bring the second works Cooper into sixth place. So the race ran its course with Clark winning by 49 seconds from Surtees. The Scot lapped everyone up to fifth place. So finished the fifth and final British Grand Prix staged at the circuit. With a total of nine events having taken place, 1962 had been the busiest season since motor racing started in 1954.

British teams and drivers preferred to spend their Easter Bank Holiday at Goodwood rather than abroad, and so it proved in 1963. They had the reigning World Champion Graham Hill, Jack Brabham in his Brabham BT3 and Bruce McLaren in the new 1963 Cooper while the British Racing Partnership entered Innes Ireland. Hill led most of the way until part of a fuel tank worked loose and blocked his supply. This let Ireland into the lead and he took the flag with McLaren just 5 seconds adrift.

Heat two of the Aintree Trophy – 'one minute to go!'

Aintree was still on the international calendar with the eighth Aintree 200 meeting on 27 April. The programme included seventeen-lap races for sports and Formula Junior cars, a ten-lap race for saloons and the fifty-lap race for Formula 1 cars. Practice was held in brilliant sunshine and ended with no less than five drivers inside the outright lap record. These were Jim Clark, Jack Brabham, Graham Hill, Innes Ireland and Richie Ginther while Clark's team-mate, Trevor Taylor, equalled the previous record. Sadly, Brabham's car suffered a broken piston and was forced to withdraw.

At the drop of the flag of the main event – to the dismay of Team Lotus – Clark failed to leave the line. The Lotus 25 was pushed into the pits to have a new battery fitted. Meanwhile, Ginther had made a superb start from the second row of the grid and had initially led, but by the end of the first lap Hill had taken the lead from Ginther who was closely followed by Ireland, McLaren, Trevor Taylor and Chris Amon. By lap eleven Clark had moved into seventh place. On lap seventeen Colin Chapman brought him in to change cars with team-mate Taylor. He then rejoined the race a minute behind the leader. Hill and Ireland were locked in a battle up front and lapping under the old lap record. However, Clark was happier in Taylor's car and began a remarkable pursuit of the leaders, breaking the lap record repeatedly. As Hill consolidated his lead over Ireland, the spectators' interest focussed on Clark's remarkable display of driving skills. Again and again he broke his own newly established lap record until he reduced it to 1 minute 51.8 seconds, at a speed of 96.60mph. Although it was not realised at the time this was to stand as the all-time lap record at the full Aintree circuit. At the flag Hill won by 15 seconds from Ireland. Clark was only 14 seconds behind Ireland in third place and he finished to a rousing reception from the spectators. At the end of the 1963 Formula 1 season, Jim Clark would be World Champion.

The BARC celebrated the reborn Palace's tenth birthday on 3 June with a 50-mile sports car race for the Crystal Palace Trophy. The Cooper Monaco of Roy Salvadori was a predictable leader for the first twenty-five laps before transmission troubles intervened. This left the blue and white Normand Lotus-Fords of Jim Clark and Mike Beckwith to finish first and second.

1963 was the first time that the start of the Tourist Trophy at Goodwood was on a normal grid as the RAC had banned Le Mans-style starts on safety grounds. First off was Graham Hill in a Ferrari GTO. Ireland was next up with Parkes (in a sister car to Hill's GTO) third and McLaren in the other Aston Martin in fourth. Parkes took the lead when Ireland and Hill had a 'moment' at Woodcote. Hill eventually reeled in his team-mate and they took a 1-2 with Roy Salvadori third in a Jaguar E-type one lap down.

The *News of the World* took over sponsorship of the feature Formula 1 race at the 1964 Easter Monday meeting at Goodwood. Every car and engine in the News of the World Trophy was British, as were the top six finishers. The BARC and Goodwood were reaping what they had sowed and the venue had played a significant role in the British motor racing renaissance as both a racing circuit and a test facility.

Graham Hill (BRM) led for most of the way with Jim Clark (Lotus) in hot pursuit. Hill seemed to have the race sorted but two laps from home a distributor broke. That led Clark through to win, followed at a distance by his team-mate Peter Arundell. The winner of the Chichester Cup for Formula 3 cars was one Jackie Stewart in a Cooper-BMC run by Ken Tyrrell. Sir Jackie recalls his relationship with the Sussex circuit:

Opposite: Jim Clark leads Graham Hill at Crystal Palace.

I first went to Goodwood with my elder brother Jimmy who was driving for Ecuria Ecosse. I was about twelve or thirteen and my autograph book was busy chasing drivers such as Mike Hawthorn, Reg Parnell and Stirling Moss for their signatures. We used to stay at the Ship Inn in Chichester because David Murray liked his creature comforts and good wine. Eventually I drove at Goodwood. I had my first ever F3 drive there and also took the Sports Car record in a Cooper. This led to the track manager Robin McKay making a recommendation to Ken Tyrrell. So in 1964 I was given a test in a works Cooper. John Cooper came down to set the times and Bruce McLaren was on track with me. I found the single-seater so precise and wonderful. There were no lap times being displayed to me and I didn't realise that I was clocking faster than Bruce. So when it was over Ken Tyrrell asked me to sign a contract and our partnership eventually led to the World Formula 1 Championship. That season I won eleven out of thirteen F3 races, including that one at Goodwood. Within a year I was racing Formula 1. So happy memories of Goodwood where I still hold the official lap record at 120.4mph.

There was a great atmosphere especially with the Duke of Richmond and Gordon around. I can remember the Duke of Edinburgh and the Duke of Kent attending our events. The downside was that while it was an unbelievably good circuit to drive on, you had to be so smooth as there were no run-off areas and you could be catapulted if you hit a bank. You had to get it right, especially with the speed built up entering Madgwick plus there were four corners which were very flat and therefore very fast. I raced a lot there before 1966 and of course it was the HQ of the BARC as well.

The final Formula 1 race to be run at Aintree took place on 18 April 1964 when the '200' race was staged. It was sixty-seven laps, having reverted to its pre-1960 format of 207 miles distance. Graham Hill took pole position in his BRM P61 and was joined at the front by Jack Brabham (Brabham BT) and Peter Arundell (Lotus 25). New Zealander Denny Hulme was the fastest of the Formula 2 runners in his works Brabham BT10.

Graham Hill took an immediate lead from Brabham and Bruce McLaren. By lap three Jim Clark, determined to make up for a poor start, was fifth. The leading three were having an intense struggle with Brabham alongside Hill and McLaren very close behind. By lap four Clark had moved into fourth place and was closing on the leaders as Brabham slipped past Hill to take the lead. Sadly, McLaren had to retire. At the end of eight laps Brabham led Hill, Clark, Arundell and Dan Gurney. The Formula 2 division of the race was equally exciting as a close struggle was also taking place between Brian Hart (Lotus), Tony Maggs (Lola) and Denny Hulme (Brabham), these three being barely a car's length apart for most of the time.

At the head of the race, Clark managed to pass Hill and closed on Brabham. Then at Tatts Corner on lap twenty-five, Clark squeezed past on the inside of Brabham to take the lead. At half distance Clark led Brabham by just 2.2 seconds with Graham Hill a further 51 seconds behind Brabham. Brabham continued to challenge Clark until he took the lead on lap forty-two. Then on lap forty-seven Clark was attempting to pass two slower cars at Melling Crossing when he found himself with no road left and ploughed into straw bales. His Lotus was wrecked and he was very lucky to emerge unhurt. As a consequence of Clark's crash, Brabham now had a strong lead over Hill. Brabham won by the comfortable margin of 34 seconds from Graham Hill who was about a minute ahead of Arundell. Following the retirement of Brian Hart, Mike Spence won the Formula 2 from Tony Maggs.

So ended an excellent day's racing which sadly was the last time that contemporary Formula 1 cars would be seen and heard at Aintree. The BARC was stunned when Mrs Topham told it emphatically that

Opposite: Graham Hill
leads at Crystal Palace
in 1964.

Opposite, far right:
Jochen Rindt, 1964.

there would be no more motor racing at Aintree after the Members' Meeting on 3 October 1964 and that demolition work would commence immediately after the 1965 Grand National meeting had taken place. This stirred the BARC into action and it immediately began negotiation with the British Racing Drivers' Club over use of Silverstone as an alternative venue for the displaced Aintree events.

There were two fundamental factors in the demise of Aintree as a major venue for motorsport. First, the decision to hold the 1964 British Grand Prix at Brands Hatch was a blow. Whether or not the RAC intended that the Grand Prix had been permanently lost is not clear, but finance was an issue. There can be little doubt it was the Grand Prix that generated the most income. In addition, by 1964 the surface of the track had deteriorated to such an extent that a significant investment, estimated at £20,000, was required for resurfacing. Also the early 1960s had brought an increasing awareness of the dangers of motor racing and the need to take positive steps to reduce the death toll and serious injuries. As a consequence the newly formed Grand Prix Drivers' Association had the improvement of driver safety as a major objective. Therefore, there is little doubt that had Aintree continued as a major motorsport venue then a significant investment in additional safety measures would have been required.

Secondly, on 1 July Mirabel Topham announced that Aintree would be sold to the Capital and Counties Property Company. The intention was that the purchaser would build a large number of houses. So followed two years of court action and a failed planning application. The uncertainty generated by these events led to the consideration that Aintree would never again feature at national and international level.

John Surtees certainly has a perspective on the track and its potential:

> As I said previously – I had ridden at Aintree as a motorcyclist. On my four-wheel debut I finished fourth in a private Cooper in an F2 race dominated by Porsche in the first three places. I set a fastest lap and Colin Chapman asked me to consider an F1 opportunity. Aintree had some fast corners then a complex before the crossings. It was a flat track but I was sorry it stopped. Mrs Topham had the vision but it was sad that it didn't develop and continue. It wasn't going to be a classic track but it was quite challenging. It had good facilities being part of the racecourse and so much more could have been made of it.

There were also shadows beginning to appear across the horizon at Crystal Palace. By 1964 the National Sports Centre was open and conflicts between the two main sports sharing the same venue began to look inevitable. At first the long-established motorsports could claim precedence over athletics but far-sighted people began to doubt if this would always be so. There were only a few Bank Holidays in the year and the dates for the major events would be bound to clash.

As well as the opening of the National Sports Centre, that year saw the arrival at the Palace of a young man to race in Formula 2 and start a meteoric climb to the heights of motorsport. Jochen Rindt was an Austrian born in 1942. At the Racing Car Show in London he placed an order for a Formula 2 Brabham. The car was ready to race over the Whitsun weekend and he took it to Mallory Park on the Sunday for his first ever race in Britain. He still finished third behind World Champion Jim Clark and his team-mate Peter Arundell. They then travelled south to compete in the London Trophy on Whit Monday, 18 May. The BARC had split the entry into two heats. The first of these was for the drivers presumed to be the fastest

and it was Jim Clark who got the initial lead but by the end of the first lap Graham Hill in the John Coombs Cooper had taken over to stay in front for the whole twenty laps. Heat two was for the 'novices' but included Peter Arundell whose car had expired on the warm-up lap of the first heat. Palace expert Alan Rees had the Roy Winkelmann Brabham on pole but next to him was Jochen Rindt in his Brabham. David Hobbs got the drop from the other front-row position and his Merlyn led for three-quarters of the first lap before Rindt came past and led all the way. The crowd eagerly awaited the final as the youngster from Austria was shaking up the top drivers. Graham Hill took pole position on the grid with Rindt and Rees completing the front row. The flag fell and Rees shot into the lead although by

29th R.A.C. INTERNATIONAL TOURIST TROPHY RACE

INCLUDING THE

SENIOR SERVICE TROPHY

RACING ORGANISED BY THE BRITISH AUTOMOBILE RACING CLUB

SATURDAY 29th AUGUST 1964

GOODWOOD

OFFICIAL PROGRAMME

2/-

lap two Hill had squeezed by. Most would have predicted his victory but Rindt took Rees on lap four and began to reduce the deficit. The leader was suffering understeer because a bracket holding the rear anti-roll bar had broken. The newcomer seized his chance to take the lead and once at the front he made no mistakes and the crowd were treated to a fine display from a driver of great promise.

At Goodwood the final running of the Tourist Trophy was this season when the event was for sportscar racers. The biggest engines in the race were 5-litre units and this was becoming a problem. Tyres were becoming wider by the month so cornering speeds were increasing and it was clear that they would increase even more.

Bruce McLaren was driving a Formula 1 Cooper with a sportscar body and a 4-litre Oldsmobile engine. He led the early laps from Dan Gurney's Cobra and Denny Hulme's Brabham BT8A-Climax. McLaren suffered a slipping clutch and Jim Clark, driving the Lotus 30, led from Hulme. Graham Hill in his Ferrari 330P came on a charge and took the lead while Clark was in the pits being refuelled. He therefore won back-to-back Tourist Trophies.

That was the end of Goodwood's running of the event. Despite stars of the calibre of Hill and Clark, the race only attracted a small crowd. Worse, there was that issue of cornering speeds. The circuit had suffered its share of serious accidents and each one had deeply affected the duke. He began to consider the future of the circuit.

The following year the Tourist Trophy transferred to Oulton Park, but the period when the TT was run at Goodwood is regarded as the Golden Age of the event.

Opposite: Towards the end of an era, a programme from one of the last meetings at Goodwood.

In the Formula 1 race at the 1965 Goodwood Easter Monday meeting, now called the Sunday Mirror Trophy, Jackie Stewart put his BRM on pole, 0.8 seconds ahead of team-mate Graham Hill and Jim Clark who had recorded an identical time to Hill. It was Hill who led from Clark during the opening laps, while Dan Gurney (Brabham) claimed third ahead of Stewart and Brabham. Clark went ahead on lap six. Stewart and Gurney retired on lap thirty-seven, having claimed second and third places which allowed Hill and Brabham to reclaim those positions. The races held under the 1,500cc Formula 1 are regarded as the greatest organised by the BARC at Goodwood. Every top team save Ferrari took part. Every top driver took part. These were drivers and their teams using the Easter Monday meeting as a dress rehearsal for the World Championship season. In a sense 1965 was the zenith of Goodwood's history but it would all be over by July 1966.

By 1965 the London County Council had become the Greater London Council, the boundaries of the capital having been widened. The new body agreed that racing should continue following its existing pattern, though the inevitable internal restructuring within the GLC brought various changes for the organisers.

Crystal Palace now had many attractions besides the motor racing and the athletics. With so many confined to a relatively small site right in the heart of one of the most densely populated areas of the country, there was some delicate balancing of priorities to be done.

31 July was the BARC National Meeting at which the Bromley Bowl for Formula 3 cars was the main race. Chris Irwin's Brabham won the heat and final.

Despite the previous controversy at Aintree, on 24 July the first of two BARC race meetings at the north-west circuit was staged. The first event was a ten-lap mixed Formula Libre/Formula 3 race which was won by the Brabham of David Bridges. In the race for GT cars, Brian Redman was victorious in the Red Rose Motors Jaguar E-type.

The final race meeting of the year was held on 2 October when the BARC organised an eight-race programme. Derek Bennett

scored wins in the Clubmans and Formula Libre races in his Chevron B1 and Brabham respectively. That was the last involvement by the BARC at national level at the circuit but a week later the BARC North-West Centre did organise the final motorsport event of the year. This was the annual Aintree Sprint measuring one mile in length and starting just before Country Corner and running clockwise to the finish, approximately half a mile down Railway Straight. For this year electronic timing was used for the first time and a speed trap was set on the last 55 yards. Freddie Smith in his Brabham BT 14 set the fastest time of the day in 44.74 seconds and recorded 134mph through the speed trap.

From the beginning of 1966 Formula 1 went from 1,500cc to 3-litre cars and when that happened non-Championship races began to disappear. Most teams were struggling to find a suitable engine for the new formula and costs also escalated so that most circuits could not pay sufficient start money to make the exercise worthwhile for the teams.

At the beginning of that year it had been announced that there would be a 3-litre limit for sportscars at Goodwood. Soon afterwards it was announced that there would be a reduced programme at the circuit.

One theory is that Freddie March was tired. Now in his sixties he was ready to hand over the running of the Goodwood Estate to his son. The old friends from Brooklands days with whom he had run Goodwod were retiring. It is said that he did not seem to have the same rapport with the new men at the BARC helm. They were, of course, from a different generation. There was also an increasing amount of bureaucracy plus the new professionalism of motor racing. The sport wasn't quite the fun that it used to be.

Before the crunch came, Goodwood had its traditional Easter Meeting. The feature race was run to Formula 2. Denny Hulme (Brabham-Honda) was quicker than Jack Brabham during qualifying but he followed the master home for a Brabham 1-2 from a field that included a total of twelve past or future World Champions on the grid. By early summer, Goodwood had closed.

GOODWOOD TO THRUXTON

The BARC Council were obviously aware of an impending problem at Goodwood as early as December 1965, for the Events Committee were asked to look into the question of alternative venues for BARC major events at that meeting. L.F. Dyer was in the chair and he was requested to write to the President of the BRDC and put forward the Council's view that a closer association between the two clubs was to be encouraged and a permanent arrangement for a BARC major meeting on Easter Monday from 1967 should be discussed.

In the next few years various venues were to come under scrutiny including Silverstone, Aintree, Castle Combe and Donington before the solution of a new permanent circuit emerged.

The process began in March 1966 when Mr Gorringe reported on the discussion with the BRDC to date. These were reported as having been on a very friendly basis and led the club to believe that for Easter Monday 1967 the BARC would be able to organise an international meeting at Silverstone on 'suitable terms'. It was also stated that, 'It could be envisaged that the BARC could in the near future be associated with the BRDC in the administration of the circuit.' It was not the only proposal for a partnership at a circuit that would come on the agenda before 1968.

By the June meeting of the Council the BARC had the international date for the Easter Monday meeting at Silverstone confirmed by the RAC, but interestingly it was suggested that a vintage meeting could be arranged for Goodwood and accordingly His Grace had appeared to favour the idea. In contrast, at the August Council meeting Mr Dyer reported that he had been informed by His Grace that it had been decided to cease the promotion of motor racing at Goodwood. The matter was discussed at length and it was agreed that Mr Dyer, Mr Lawry, Mr Clarke and Mr MacBeth should produce a suitable press announcement from the BARC which should coincide with the public announcement that was to be made by the Goodwood Road Racing Company. It was agreed that Mr Dyer would write to His Grace expressing the regrets of the Council at his decision.

Mr Sinclair then asked if an approach could be made to Mrs Topham regarding the future use of Aintree. It was agreed that Mr Dyer should contact her and discuss the possibility of using the circuit in 1967.

Mr Sinclair was obviously keen on the idea, for at the September 1966 Council meeting he enquired what progress had been made with Mrs Topham and the Aintree circuit as he had been informed that dates for meetings had been agreed with clubs in the area. Mr Dyer reported that he had written to Mrs Topham asking for news of the position of motor racing relative to the BARC. Mrs Topham had replied that before they gave thought to further meetings she would require details of the expenses involved in bringing the circuit into line with present requirements. Mr MacBeth had written giving details of what the BARC considered to be necessary and awaited a reply from Mrs Topham. Mr Sinclair urged that the matter was pressed and so it was agreed that Mr Sinclair would be given permission to discuss with Mrs Topham the possibility of meetings organised by the BARC taking place on the club or full circuit in 1967. This eventually led to no progress on the issue at all and by the Council meeting of 7 February 1967 another circuit came under consideration. Mr Gorringe reported that he and Mr Lawry had received an invitation from Mr Delamont of the RAC to lunch with Mr John Danny to discuss Donington. This was duly discussed and it was agreed that at present Mr Gorringe and Mr Lawry should listen to any proposals and report back to the Council. This led to a Special Meeting of the Council by 27 February. Mr Dyer in the chair thanked members for attending the meeting at short notice and stressed the necessity for strict acceptance by members of the confidential nature of the information that was to be given and discussed.

Mr Gorringe reviewed a luncheon meeting and subsequent talks that had taken place during the previous two weeks involving Mr John Danny (Grovewood Securities), Mr John Webb (Motor Circuit Developments), Mr Dean Delamont (RAC), Mr Dixon (ACU) plus Mr Gorringe and Mr Lawry (BARC). The BARC had been informed of the proposed development by Grovewood Securities of Donington and the plans that this company had in mind for the promotion of motor racing at this circuit in 1968. The BARC had been offered the opportunity of taking a financial interest in the project at 'par' but this could be considered later in the negotiations. Grovewood Securities had asked that the BARC give consideration to a programme that would give them a 'home' at a circuit which could become one of the finest in Great Britain. It had been suggested that the BARC organise their international meetings at Easter, Whitsun and the 200, plus four public meetings and as many club meetings as they felt capable of organising. The BARC would be paid a fee plus a percentage of the profits for the international meetings and a share of the gate at the club meetings. The BARC would be the major organisers at this circuit and the BRSCC would not organise any international meetings there at all. No extension of the crowded major calendar was envisaged by the RAC and this was supported by all those present at the luncheon.

Mr Gorringe gave a breakdown of the estimated profits that the club could expect if the project was successfully developed and this showed an overall annual income from the one circuit as being an estimated £10,000 allowing for loss of profits at other circuits. No restriction would be imposed on the club regarding other circuits, apart from the agreement that the BARC would not be invited to organise international meetings at Brands Hatch. A ten-year agreement with an option to continue had been suggested and accepted as a reasonable period for consideration.

The club had been pressed to give an early indication of interest in the project as Grovewood Securities had to make a final decision soon. If the answer was no then they wouldn't consider the project any more. If yes, they would finally decide within ten days. Mr Lawry confirmed the proposals outlined by Mr Gorringe and added that he was in sympathy with the scheme and felt that it would bring new life into the club after the recent setbacks suffered.

Mr Dyer explained that he had written to the Hon. G. Lascelles (BRDC) stating the position that they were being asked to discuss Donington relative to the BARC and asking if any progress could be expected on the proposed amalgamation of interests in the BARC/BRDC at Silverstone. The Hon. G. Lascelles had not been able to answer as he was out of the country but Mr John Eason Gibson had replied personally and had stated that no immediate move could be made and that no move could be anticipated in 1967.

During the subsequent discussion several points were made. Firstly, that the BARC had been invited to enjoy the opportunity at Donington because they had the available dates. Secondly, that if they said yes only to find that the project was not then going ahead then great harm could be done to ongoing relations with the BRDC. There would be no official communication to the BRDC until a firm answer came from Grovewood Securities. If Grovewood Securities said yes, the press announcement would need to be agreed with the BARC, preferably after Easter Monday.

Mr Browning was concerned that because of the growing control that one financial group had in the field of motor racing in Great Britain, a decision to go to Donington could be right for the present interests of the BARC but not of necessity in the future interests of the sport.

Finally Mr Gordon England proposed, and Mr Sinclair seconded, that, 'The Council are grateful for the negotiations to date and agree that they would like them to proceed.' This was agreed unanimously.

However, on 11 April Mr Gorringe had to advise the Council that he had been informed that Grovewood Securities were not proceeding with the development of Donington Park and that negotiations relative to this matter had ceased. So on 24 April 1967 the question of a circuit for the BARC to use as a home was further discussed at a meeting of the Development Committee. Mr Clarke advised the meeting that the Council were very conscious of this need and projects were always open to serious consideration. It had recently been hoped that a particular circuit would have been available but it had not been possible and even at this time another circuit was under preliminary discussion. Castle Combe was not yet to be discounted as a possible home and even though its location would limit the interest to a particular area, this must apply to most circuits. To purchase and own a circuit would need a considerable capital investment and backing – this was not an easy problem to surmount. It was agreed to recommend that the Council should publicise the fact that they were working on schemes to replace Goodwood in order to keep the membership advised.

Within days there came a first mention of the Thruxton circuit in Hampshire at a meeting of the Finance and General Purposes Committee (2 May 1967). Mr Clarke reported that the question of the venue being used again was being discussed. He had seen a Mr Woodhouse who, together with a Mr Pelham, was understood to be a principal in the present ownership. Grovewood Securities had an offer in for the site but Mr Woodhouse had stated that at present he was not decided on the future and if they decided to develop the site themselves they would like the answers to two questions: would the BARC be prepared to organise motor racing at Thruxton and would they also assist in the management of the circuit? It is interesting to note that Mr Lawry felt that the development of the circuit would be best in the hands of Grovewood Securities but the matter was left for further reports.

A week later the Thruxton situation was discussed by the Council. Mr Fisk was concerned that the club did not lose the goodwill of Mr Woodhouse by appearing disinterested in his tentative proposals. Other members of the Council considered that the club should not upset the position with Grovewood Securities by trying to deal with both sides. On a vote it was decided that the Council would prefer to organise races at Thruxton with the circuit ownership in the hands of Grovewood Securities. It was agreed to approach John Webb and try to ascertain his intentions and at the same time sound his views on the BARC organising at Thruxton if it remained an independently owned circuit.

At the June Council meeting Mr Clarke reported that to date no definite decision had been made on Thruxton but he understood that Motor Circuits Development were still making enquiries and Mr Webb had indicated that he hoped the circuit would be available for Easter Monday 1968. The BARC had also discussed a circuit layout with Mr Woodhouse who, at that time, had not had an offer from Motor Circuit Developments and who welcomed the BARC interest in the motor racing side of the circuit should his company decided to develop the site themselves. By the end of that month the Finance and General Purposes Committee had held a long discussion with the owners of the freehold of Thruxton and exchanged views with regard to the possibility of the club organising racing at this venue at some time in the future. That was reported to the Council in July. It was not possible to report on further development but it was agreed that a Circuit Development Committee should be formed. It was thought that this committee would enable Mr Clarke to deal quickly with matters.

At the first meeting on 24 July the offer made by Mr Woodhouse giving the club the opportunity to promote motorsport at Thruxton was discussed fully. Several points of detail emerged which needed further discussion with Mr Woodhouse and a letter was sent to him outlining the points which were considered important at that stage. Subsequently a second meeting was arranged. At that meeting on 31 July, after a frank discussion on the many aspects of the proposals made by Mr Woodhouse and the points raised in the letter, it was agreed that the owners would prepare the circuit at their expense and arrange for work to be carried out to the satisfaction of the RAC and arrange for the necessary facilities to be available to enable a major race meeting to be organised by the BARC on Easter Monday 1968 and that work was to be completed prior to 1 March 1968 to enable the club to run club meetings before the Easter meeting if necessary. The club would be invited to appoint two directors to an operating company. The operating company would be jointly owned by the BARC and the owners of Thruxton on a 49/51 basis, with a share capital of £100. The BARC would have the 49 per cent share and would undertake to supply the management of the operating company in order to facilitate the speed of operation that would be necessary. The initial working capital for this company would be supplied on loan by the freeholders.

The financial and working agreements for this co-operative venture were such that the BARC would not be called on to supply any working capital for the fixed items, buildings and land, but would be expected through the operating company to supply certain moveable items necessary for the running of a race meeting. The operating company would be responsible for all circuit and promotional matters connected with the running of the circuit for motor racing, etc. The BARC would be responsible for the organisation of the race meetings run under their name.

In August it was recommended that Mr S.M. Lawry and Mr R.L. Clarke should be the directors appointed by the BARC. It was also agreed that Mr Clarke be seconded to the operating company as General Manager of the company. It was understood that for some considerable time this would necessitate Mr Clarke acting in a dual capacity and that was considered necessary at that stage to expedite the circuit development. By the time of a Finance and General Purposes Committee meeting on 30 October Mr Clarke was able to report that work had started on the earthworks and that road surfacing would be started in the near future. So with a mammoth effort from the contractors, the whole 2.356-mile perimeter circuit was resurfaced, spectator banks built, marshals' posts constructed and pits plus race control built.

On 6 February 1968 at the Events Committee, Mr Lawry read letters that he had received from Mrs Allard and Lady Segrave, both of whom were very pleased that corners should be named after their late husbands. As yet no reply had been received from Mrs Cobb and Lady Campbell.

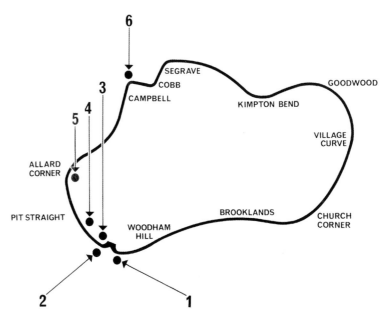

A circuit map of Thruxton.

It was stressed by the Committee that the first meeting, to be run on 17 March, should not run to too tight a time schedule. Mr White reported that the regulations for this meeting had been distributed and that owing to a church service, the practice time was restricted which really determined the number of races that could be run. Mr White gave a brief outline of how the local church services would affect practice and said that the club had been in contact with the local vicar.

The very first race on Sunday 17 March 1968 was for Special Saloons up to 1 litre and was won by Chichester's Alistair McHardy in his Hillman Imp. The first international meeting followed very quickly when Easter Monday heralded the first Thruxton Formula 2 race. Jochen Rindt won that day and completed a hat-trick over the next two years as some of the finest drivers made Easter Monday at Thruxton a famous event. Geoffrey Charles, motoring correspondent of *The Times*, described that first outing:

26-year-old Jochen Rindt, currently one of the world's fastest Grand Prix drivers, who has just joined Jack Brabham's Formula One team for the 1968 World Championship series, fought a 130mph battle at Thruxton yesterday to drive his 1.6-litre Brabham-Ford to victory against a hair-raising challenge by Jean-Pierre Beltoise of France.

Beltoise, a former French motorcycle racing champion, who won last weekend's tragic Hockenheim Formula 2 race in which World Champion Jim Clark was killed, almost won yesterday's big race which was organised by the British Automobile Racing Club and watched by a crowd of 45,000. Rindt had one of the hardest battles of his career. He was hounded throughout by the little dark-haired Frenchman who is in his first year of Grand Prix racing with the new French Matra team.

Above: Lord Howe in a 1953 Alfa Romeo officially opens the circuit.

Above right: Jochen Rindt, F2 winner at the official opening of Thruxton.

Right: An advert in the 40th anniversary programme, reproduced from 1968.

The
BRITISH AUTOMOBILE RACING CLUB

"MOTOR RACING AT ITS BEST"

WHATEVER YOUR INTEREST IN THE SPORT OF MOTOR RACING - OR IN ANY OF THE ASSOCIATED SPORTING ACTIVITIES OF THE MOTORING ENTHUSIAST, YOU WILL BENEFIT BY BEING A MEMBER OF THE B.A.R.C

RACING, AUTOCROSS, SPRINTS, RALLIES, HILL CLIMBS, CONTESTS, COURS, DRIVING GYMKHANAS & SOCIAL EVENTS.

WRITE FOR FULL DETAILS:
B.A.R.C
THRUXTON CIRCUIT, ANDOVER HAMPSHIRE, SP11 8PN
TELEPHONE: 01264 882200

Beltoise, driving his light-blue Formula 2 Matra-Ford, finished second with Derek Bell of Britain third in a Brabham-Ford. Rindt's winning time in the fifty-four-lap final of the three-part Thruxton Trophy race over the 2.4-mile twisting Hampshire circuit was 1 hour 9 minutes 45.6 seconds, an average of 109.42mph. This was a new all-out circuit record, though it was the first international race meeting on this new circuit. Rindt also made the fastest lap in 1 minute 16 seconds (111.6 mph).

The Thruxton racing proved that this is certainly one of the fastest circuits in Europe and the BARC deserve congratulations for their organisation from start to finish of the five-race programme.

Plenty of memories were in store over the forthcoming decades at the Hampshire circuit, but not that many years after the gain of a new circuit for the BARC had come the loss of another.

11

SAFETY FIRST

When the 1960s came to a close at Crystal Palace, the decade had seen a great deal of change. Not only had the venue been transformed by the arrival of the National Sports Centre but motor racing had changed too, becoming far more professional. The impact of both sponsorship and rapid technical development produced a far-reaching shift in standards and attitudes.

Those changes in the world of motorsport were evident as the new decade opened. Large-budget advertising was setting the style at international level and the days of the private entrant in anything above club level were numbered. The cars and bikes were enveloped in major sponsors' colour schemes and logos. There were other changes too. The question of safety was receiving much more attention than before, partly as a result of recent fatalities. Circuit owners and organisers were being required to do much more to protect competitors and spectators alike and the ever-rising speeds achieved by increasingly sophisticated racing machinery made the task an even more demanding one. The Grand Prix Drivers' Association, under the leadership of Jackie Stewart, called for the installation of many more safety fences and crash barriers, plus the removal of hazards like earth banks and trees that were too close to the track. Crystal Palace obviously could not escape the attention of the drivers, particularly as it staged international meetings, and any safety measures incorporated for the professional competitors would benefit the clubmen as well. However, it was going to cost a great deal of money. The GLC had a limited budget for leisure amenities and as the demand for money for safety measures at the circuit grew, so did the feeling in the GLC hierarchy that perhaps motorsport at the Palace was coming to an end.

The drivers had inspected the circuit and their representative François Cevert, Tyrrell Grand Prix driver and team-mate to Jackie Stewart, felt that an armco barrier should be erected on the inside of North Tower Crescent. The management did not relish the idea of a steel structure so close to the Concert Bowl. Cevert suggested a demountable barrier but when it was disclosed that the cost of this and other safety measures would be about £250,000 there was a sharp intake of breath at the GLC.

Mike Hawthorn leads Jody Scheckter at Crystal Palace in 1972.

Despite all this, the court injunction imposed on the circuit in 1953 had expired by 1970 and the GLC decided that more meetings could be promoted increasing the permitted days for racing from five to fourteen.

However, a few weeks before the beginning of the 1972 season came the inevitable announcement from the GLC Arts and Recreation Committee. After the season was over Crystal Palace would no longer stage motor racing. Many reasons were put forward for the closure and some of them had been evident for a long time, but it was still a very sad turn of events for the Palace enthusiasts, particularly in view of the recent increased activity at the circuit.

The final international race meeting at the Palace was held by the BARC on Monday 29 May 1972 and it was the fifth round of the European Formula 2 Championship. The atmosphere was rather downbeat with closure looming, but the quality of the entry ensured that the circuit would go out on a high note.

The Chairman of the GLC Arts and Recreation Committee, H. Sebag-Montefiore wrote of the impending closure in the programme and circuit manager Allan Tyler contributed a review of past seasons.

Local hero John Surtees was making a welcome return to the circuit, not having raced there since 1967. He was now the constructor as well as the driver of his own cars. Mike Hailwood joined fellow former motorcycle racer John Surtees in his team. Mike was racing at the Palace on four wheels for the first time, not having visited the circuit since 1957.

Heat one saw a comfortable victory for Carlos Reutemann after pole-sitter John Surtees packed up in the lead during the seventh lap. The Argentinian in the Rondel Racing Brabham had gone through the field to achieve his victory. Heat two saw François Cevert in the Elf March on pole. Eventually Mike Hailwood took the chequered flag with Jody Scheckter in the works Impact McLaren in second place.

Sixteen Formula 2 finalists now were ready to do battle. Scheckter led away with Hailwood and Reutemann in pursuit through North Tower. By lap thirteen Hailwood was hounding Scheckter and the crowd were in support as he found a way past. However, a broken anti-roll bar was causing Mike severe handling problems. Seven laps from home the Surtees and McLaren were nose to tail. On lap forty-seven the cars were side by side past the pits with Scheckter on the outside round the kink before North Tower and he was able to outbrake Hailwood into the turn and accelerate into the Glade ahead. Mike could do no more and had to be content with second place, although he had some consolation in having set the fastest lap during his heat – 48.4 seconds, 103.39mph. This was the outright record which would stand for all time. The crowd were captivated and the Palace reputation for close and exciting racing was being maintained to the last.

For the car-racing fans there were just a couple more meetings. On 9 September the BARC arrived with the Hexagon Trophy meeting. At this event Formula 3 was the main attraction. Mike Walker was the last Formula 3 winner at the Palace; his works Ensign was some way ahead of Peter Hull's Brabham.

When the final day arrived with the staging of an historic car meeting on Saturday 23 September 1972, the Hon. Gerald Lascelles wrote an appreciation in the programme recalling that the Crystal Palace track:

> . . . has filled a unique role in British racing history. It is the only circuit owned by a municipality and the only one sited within the confines of a major city. With hindsight one could argue, with a touch of irony, that these two factors contributed most to the decision to close the circuit. Modern racing machinery, for all its advanced sophistication, does not generate the quietest scene on Earth. Nor does its greatly enhanced speed factor ease the problem of the circuit owner in containing the cars from the public viewing areas. With these factors weighing heavily against its retention, it was perhaps inevitable that a council not over orientated in motorsport enthusiasm should take the decision to close the track.

That decision is not one looked back on favourably by two British motorsport icons. John Surtees comments:

Murray Walker.

It was basically stopped by the introduction of athletics. The fact that motor racing was the only profitable part of the Crystal Palace set-up was ignored. It was a unique circuit. It had character and history.

Murray Walker adds:

I used to go to Crystal Palace quite a lot to commentate for the BBC on radio and on television. It was a bloody good circuit. To be thoroughly contentious – I strongly resent the closure of Crystal Palace. While I have got nothing against athletics as a sport and a lot of people get a lot of enjoyment out of it – the British motorsport industry contributes a gigantic amount to our economy. We are world leaders in motorsport and I believe that the industry employs 50,000 people. We generate an enormous amount of business and exports. Athletics certainly doesn't do that. A pity, for nowadays for everything up to and including Formula 3 and Touring Cars it would still be a cracking circuit.

12

EXPANSION

So Thruxton was to prove to be the long-term base for the BARC, but life wasn't exactly smooth-running at the Hampshire circuit. During the summer of 1970 the use of the venue was challenged by the county council. A public enquiry ruled that it could only be used for racing on twenty-one days each year. When this was challenged by local objectors, the BARC reached an out-of-court settlement limiting racing to twelve days each year, a situation that remains to this day.

Murray Walker certainly has a view on this:

I have always felt very aggrieved about the fact that the BARC have never been able, in my opinion, to exploit its position of strength as much as it could have or should have done at Thruxton because they are not allowed to race as much as they should be. Thruxton is bloody spectacular. God knows how many days of my life I have spent at Thruxton. Not just for the cars but for the bikes.

By the time that Jochen Rindt raced at Thruxton over the Easter Weekend 1970, he was an established Grand Prix star, but Formula 2 was for fun. It was a chance to race away from the Formula 1 pressures. So he thrilled a massive Easter Monday crowd with a display of consummate talent.

As the summer of 1970 developed, Rindt was unstoppable on the Grand Prix scene. Tragically, qualifying for the Italian GP in early September he crashed at 150mph and was killed. He became the first posthumous World Champion, for the points total that he amassed was not beaten. In memory of an outstanding driver there was commissioned a special trophy. In 1971 it was presented to the winner of the race that Rindt had made his own in the three previous years. Inaugural winner of the trophy was Graham Hill. Right up to 1985 Thruxton continued to host a Formula 2 race on Easter Monday. Winners of the Jochen Rindt Trophy included future Formula 1 stars Ronnie Peterson, Jacques Lafitte and Johnny Cecotto.

Sir Jackie Stewart has experience of the circuit and a perspective on his fellow World Champion: 'Thruxton is extraordinarily fast. I did a lot of F2 for Matra and Brabham there. It was not Goodwood for

Above: A sports car race entering Campbell Corner, Thruxton, in July 1968.

Right: The delights of spectating!

atmosphere, but Graham Hill and Jochen Rindt raced there a lot in different formulae. Jochen was the man to beat in those days.'

John Surtees was aware of the improvements after 1968:

The BARC eventually moved into Thruxton and changes did take place. I had raced there against the then World Motorcycle Champion Geoff Duke on my Vincent. The back section was similar but they made a change to the loop. There are decent quick corners at Thruxton and that helps driver development. We raced F2 at Thruxton with Mike Hailwood at the wheel. Thruxton has the problem that many airfield circuits have of being flat, but it has a down section at the back. Overall it is a good challenge.

Former Grand Prix driver and current Chief Executive of Motor Sport Vision, Dr Jonathan Palmer, recalls his early knowledge of both the BARC and the Thruxton circuit:

Above left: As Murray Walker says, Thruxton is not only for cars but also for bikes.

Above: Jackie Stewart at Thruxton.

Historic racing, Thruxton, 1975.

Formula Ford, Thruxton, 1977.

Opposite: A common sight at circuits such as Thruxton – a Jim Russell training school, 1977.

Above: Jonathan Palmer.

As a teenager I was desperate to be taken to watch motor racing but my GP father said that if he was going to take me he'd at least go as a circuit doctor and be useful. He contacted the BARC, became a medical officer and soon Chief Medical Officer for the BARC. He became great friends with Sidney Offord, the BARC's Executive Director, no doubt through their enjoyment of a glass or two of wine and I suspect that helped me a bit when I started racing as an ambitious eighteen-year-old medical student!

My first ever race was at Thruxton in 1975 in an Austin-Healey Sprite and the following year I moved up to a Marcos 3-litre, still in the club sports car championship. I could only afford a half-share in the Marcos but won first time out at Thruxton. My co-owner was so thrilled to see his car have its first race win that he said he wouldn't drive after all and just enjoy watching me race it!

Thruxton is a great circuit. I used to love racing there. It is fast and flowing. The first corner – Allard – is pretty quick, and then you have the great sequence of Campbell, Cobb and Segrave, where line is critical, particularly for racecraft. Then you head out the back for the ballsy fast-sweeping Kimpton, Goodwood and Church corners – drivers love the challenge of nearly flat-out bends.

Jonathan Palmer in a Ralt Honda.

My 1981 championship-winning F3 year saw mixed fortunes at Thruxton. I had an early season win and then we were back there for round five after I had won the first four races on the trot. With the BBC and Murray Walker coming to Thruxton to follow my mercurial form, the pressure was on for a fifth straight win. Inevitably it came to a spectacular end on TV when I got taken out at Campbell on the first lap! But overall I've happy memories of racing at Thruxton.

It was a great honour for me to receive the BARC Gold Medal in 1983 for winning the European F2 Championship, made all the more special because of my history with the BARC. I was very proud, particularly given the illustrious names that preceded me and I still have my medal on my trophy shelves, though the ribbon is a bit faded now!

Thruxton eventually celebrated its twenty-fifth anniversary in October 1993 when Damon Hill set a blistering unofficial lap record by achieving a time of 57.6 seconds at a speed of 147.25mph during a demonstration drive in the Williams Renault FW 15C.

By this time Sidney Offord, who had joined the BARC in 1975, had handed over the reins to a new Chief Executive, Dennis Carter. Sidney's contribution is well remembered by his successor:

Sidney employed me actually. I had met Warwick Offord, his son, who was the circuit manager at Thruxton in the mid-1980s. Through Warwick I started to get involved in the BARC. I was already involved in motor racing. I got involved with a couple of BARC events that they did such as the Beaujolais Rally. I also started, believe it or not, to drive a breakdown truck at Thruxton on their behalf. I got to know Sid, his father, and later it was Sid that asked me to come here. Sid was very much a larger-than-life character. You did as you were told. His phrase was: 'If you don't like it – there's the door.' My comment on the view that Sidney turned the financial affairs of the BARC around is that it is certainly true. I don't think that Sidney was a financial genius, I would never say that. What he was very good at was realising where the leaks were. Shortly before Sidney came – if you look back at the history of the club then – we had reached a point where the Council and the club were spending more money than they earned. There was probably nobody in the club who was brave enough to stand up and say, 'You can't do this. You have got to cut your cloth to match your income.' Sid was certainly brave enough to do that. Sid was very much, 'If you are not earning it then you don't spend it.' He did bring the whole of the club's financial matters under control in that way. His family business was bakeries and restuarants in Southend. He had a history of motorsport with TEAC – the Thames Estuary Automobile Club. Sid was one of the people who invented Rallycross for television. It just took off and became very popular.

My own background was very much retail and commerce. Just prior to coming to Thruxton I had been Retail Development Director for Imperial Tobacco. Imperial Tobacco were then bought out by Hanson Trust. I was asked if I would carry on but for various reasons I didn't. For a year I just worked as a consultant for various businesses around the city and around the country. I was then approached by Warwick Offord on behalf of Sid because the BARC were looking for a competitions director. I was obviously well into motorsport. I was competing in clubmen's cars or sportscars. I did race at Thruxton – badly! Of course I didn't have a full-time job so I came down and saw Sid and Michael Groves. I went home and said to Hazel, my wife, 'Great job, but there is no way that I'm going to do it because there's no money.' She said that as I was pretty fed up with commerce why not do it for a year or two and then go back to commerce afterwards? So, I came to the BARC headquarters at Thruxton as Competitions Director. I went there in February 1988 and it involved putting together the competition programme, looking after all the entries and the marshalling force plus running testing. My move from Competitions Director to Chief Executive within a relatively short space of time is interesting. Sid by then was seventy – he was well past his retiring date. He also had problems with his eyesight and was going blind. I used to have to drive him. It was a difficult time actually because not only was I trying to run competitions but if Sid was going anywhere for a meeting then I had to take him because there was no way that he could drive himself.

Sidney Offord on the left.

Dennis Carter.

Phil Davies.

In the interim period I had decided that it had been a great job but I was offered a lot of money to go back to industry. So I handed my notice in. Council at that point then decided, rightly or wrongly, to ask me to go for an interview as Chief Executive. I nearly said no. I thought – they've seen me for eighteen months so why do they want to interview me? It was Michael Groves who actually said, 'Play the game'. So I did.

That was 1990. The year we acquired the lease on Pembrey and I did all the negotiations. I can't claim the original contact with the local authority. That was Sidney. Llanelli Borough Council had built this race circuit which obviously seemed a good idea to them at the time, but they really didn't know what to do with it. They didn't know how to get it licensed. They didn't know how to run it. So when I arrived Sid was just starting to give them advice. So I got that job – going to talk to them and giving them the advice on what they should and shouldn't be doing. Initially they didn't licence it for car racing. It was used for motorcycle racing in the same way that the ACU had licensed a lot of airfields.

So I pick up the negotiations. We start to advise them and they say that they now want to licence it for car racing. So we take them through all of the steps to license it with the MSA. They do that and they get the circuit licensed. Then they decide they want to run some race meetings. Again, they don't know how to go about it. I said, 'Why don't we run them on your behalf?' In 1989 – for one year only – we did a management contract with them. We managed their race meeting for them over the twelve months. We put the calendar together and we oversaw the race meetings, even if we were not specifically running them. At the end of the year they came to me, having seen what's happened for a year, and said, 'There is no way we can pick up that from you. So we are going to put up the site for tender.' That's what they did. The site went up for tender and we applied for it alongside other organisations. We were successful and we did take over the staff that the local authority had there. Phil Davies wasn't one of them. We employed Phil as a separate entity and he's still there!

Circuit Manager Phil Davies takes up the tale of the West Wales venue:

Before 1990 Pembrey was a basic airfield runway with a shortened version of the circuit – a mile circuit. It was totally flat with no real spectator areas. They had to be put up prior to events. The paddock area was totally on the outside and there was one Portakabin toilet and that basically was that. As I said it was totally flat and at that time prone to flooding. Obviously over the years we have been working on the drainage and that has improved. I came on board as Circuit Manager the day we took the lease over – which was 4 January 1990. When I ran motorcycle meetings prior to the BARC days I used to bring a double-decker bus down for race control facilities, etc. One of the first things I did was to go up to the local bus company to see if they had a spare double-decker bus. So that was here on a permanent basis before we built the race control and the scrutineering bay.

With respect to events staged – it's a strange one. The more facilities we have put in, the less of the bigger events we have run. In the early 1990s we were running British Superbikes and British Touring Cars. Matters changed within the structure of those events and we lost them.

With respect to the many Formula 1 teams and drivers who have tested here – obviously we are a bit out of the way although people believe we are further away than we actually are. We do run quite a tight ship and if the teams asked for privacy then we gave them privacy. There isn't a name in Formula 1 who hasn't been to Pembrey. The nature of the circuit itself – the layout – just lends itself for driver development. The circuit is fast and slow but you've got – apart from a mile-long straight – every variety from left-handers to right-handers. You ask anybody in motorsport in the world where the Honda curve is and they will tell you Pembrey. It's that sort of bend. It's all quite challenging for the teams and that's why they liked it.

This was one of Ayrton Senna's favourite tracks for testing. He is probably one of the greatest drivers in the past thirty years without any question. He enjoyed

Ayrton Senna.

a challenge and he set an unofficial F1 lap record at Pembrey at 40.7 seconds. It was a phenomenal achievement knocking seconds off what everybody else was going around in. So that's why Ayrton liked the circuit. The challenge was there and it pushed him as a driver.

The first time Michael Schumacher drove the Jordan to its potential was at Pembrey. They did all the PR at Silverstone – all the glory of his pulling out of the pit lane. They did a lap and then put it back in the truck and came down here for two or

Michael Schumacher.

three days to test the car. You could see there was something special about the guy. Michael had a good team around him. Gary Anderson at the time was the man in Formula 1 with respect to engineering and concepts. So they worked together very well.

The 1990s saw us busy with the F1 teams but then politics took over. There was a change of rules and it restricted the amount of testing they could do and restricted the venues they could go to.

The BARC kept us going for the first ten years and we've turned all that around. We've been standing on our own two feet quite healthily for the last ten years. Like Croft we had a noise problem and it went to court. It went our way and we won our case. That was 2007. 50 per cent of our business is in midweek and the other 50 per cent is on the weekend. We do run our own driving experiences but that's on a fairly low scale compared to Thruxton. We operate our driving school on a Sunday when I haven't got anything else on. It's used for PR to bring people in who wouldn't normally come to Pembrey. We might even get some racing drivers out of it – which we have in the past.

We are balanced between car events and bike events. We obviously run all the BARC Championships and the Truck Racing Championships which the BARC has taken under its wing. Pembrey is a natural home for the trucks and they come here at least twice a year. So we normally run an early event and a late event. They are obviously big vehicles but are restricted to 100mph. We have got two quite quick straights but the rest of it is quite demanding so the trucks on the circuit are sideways half the time. Good for the spectators!

We have always been known as the home of Welsh Motorsport. To be fair to Dennis he does say that's what we are. We are a motorsport centre and we must continue with what we do including the rallies, rallycross and the other varieties. However, it would be nice to have a big event again.

We have put a new pitlane in during the last couple of years. In 2011 we upgraded a lot of the paddock facilities. Probably after 2012 we need to be looking at resurfacing again. Maintenance is a huge investment on its own. Recently we have put new spectator fencing up and increased our spectator area. Some of the areas that we have got now are the best in British motorsport. We haven't got big grandstands but we can park thousands of cars on the banks so that fans can watch from their vehicles.

Truck racing.

After Pembrey came Mallory Park and the following press release was issued on 12 January 2005:

BARC Ltd are delighted to announce the purchase of Mallory Park (Motor Sport) Ltd. The acquisition of Mallory Park (Motor Sport) Ltd will entitle the BARC Ltd to full operational rights of the superb Leicestershire circuit. The former pony-trekking site, bought by the late Clive Wormleighton, and converted into a tarmac circuit in the 1950s, has largely retained its original concept and layout – a fast, simple venue that provides spectacular motor racing. Because of this, Mallory Park has seen some of the greatest names in motorsport, either on two or four wheels. Such a great history and the undoubted potential of the venue have made the Leicestershire circuit an obvious choice for the BARC.

Sportmaxx at Pembrey.

The purchase of Mallory Park will take the club's tally of circuits to three, the BARC running both the Thruxton circuit since the late 1960s and Pembrey since the early 1990s.

The BARC Ltd had been contemplating purchasing another circuit for some time and to acquire such a prestigious venue is great news for the club.

Mallory Park's Managing Director David Overend stated:

I am delighted that agreement has been reached regarding the future of Mallory Park. My family have been involved with the circuit for over thirty years, since 1984 as day-to-day operators. The decision to move on was not an easy one but both Ron and I are convinced that Mallory Park will prosper with the BARC and that the circuit's traditions and style will continue under their guidance.

Dennis Carter takes up the story:

With Mallory Park we had a long history of putting meetings on. I was always close to the Overend family – Edwina in particular. Edwina was Mallory Park to me. She was a personality. She was another larger-than-life character. Motorsport in those days had quite a lot of them. The Sidney Offords, the John Webbs and Edwina. I really liked Edwina but I liked the family as well. David we never saw so much until after Edwina's death. David, when he came in to run the business, while he made a good job of it – I don't think his heart was really in it in the same way as it had been for his mother and father.

After Edwina died we began to talk about the fact that they might consider selling. I remember having dinner with Ron and David at the RAC in Pall Mall. I think we virtually agreed a price that night. Then we continued to talk about it and put

Below left: Pembrey circuit.

Below: Mallory Park circuit.

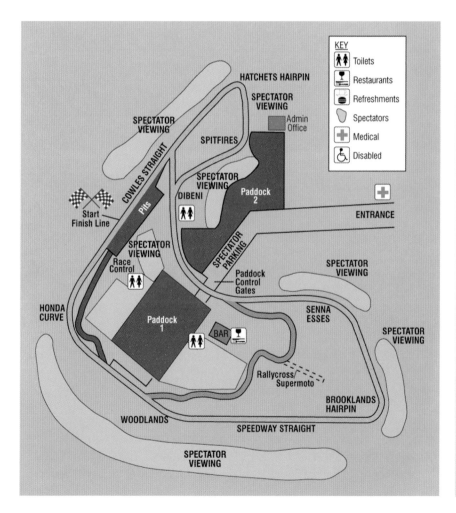

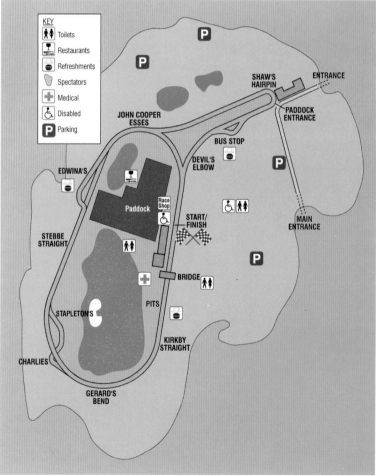

139

the deal together. From the BARC point of view it was about expansion. I had always felt, and to a certain extent still do, that the job of running motor racing at a club unless you own the venue is going to get harder and harder. We needed more venues. To just have Thruxton, which we did when I first came to the BARC, was never going to be enough. So previously the Pembrey situation had been a real opportunity and we had had some good years. We had developed, we had become bigger, we had become stronger. We were now wealthy enough to go out and make things happen. So when the Mallory situation came up we could afford to take it on. It was something we felt that we wanted to do and it was a well-located facility.

I'm really pleased with Mallory. We have totally resurfaced it including the paddock. There must be people cheering in motorsport that we have finally tarmacked the Mallory paddock! Circuit Manager John Ward is the one who finds something to do. He will always find a hole to dig somewhere. Usually something that makes a mess.

We bought the lease and part of any deal is to make sure that the landlord is happy with you as tenant. In fairness to ex-racing driver Chris Meek he was happy that the BARC was going to be the tenant. He appears to be happy with the direction that the circuit is going.

As circuit manager John Ward confirms:

So [there have been] a lot of improvements over the last couple of years. Still a few years of ideas to come yet. For example, we have always had a motocross track here. Then working with the local community we moved the track further away from the village – another 70 to 80 metres away. We restructured the circuit so the machines are not accelerating in the direction of the village, so the noise goes the other way. That track we use for half a dozen motocross events throughout the year. It is also used for testing twice a month. In 2008 and 2009 we ran the British Grand Prix round of the World Championship – a massive event and really successful . . . very well attended with over 40,000 present. In 2009 we also ran a round of the World Super-Moto Championships at the same time which used the track and the modified areas on the run-offs. That was almost done as entertainment for the motocross because it ran Friday evening and Saturday evening which again proved very successful and the spectators had a full weekend of motorcycle sport.

What that led to was running a round of the British Championship in 2010. We have also run a round of the four-stroke championship and the twin-shock championship. We brought those back in 2011 and for 2012 we are looking at staging one of the Red Bull rounds as well. Mallory Park is now becoming a motorsport centre rather than just Mallory Park race circuit. My aim when I came was to turn it into a venue rather than a racetrack.

Opposite top: John Ward.

Opposite bottom: Resurfacing at Mallory Park.

Left: Motocross at Mallory Park.

Above: Supermoto at Mallory Park.

Above right: An Abba tribute concert at Mallory Park.

I would like to do some more outside events. We have done a few pop concerts. We did a day with Triumph in 2010 when they celebrated twenty years of manufacturing motorcycles in Hinckley. They had a day on the track and in the evening a pop concert with Mumford and Sons. They were supported by the original Stranglers. So we had the modern and the old. That was a great evening with over 8,000 people on site for the pop concert.

After the Super-Moto event we had an approach from the British Rallycross Championship – could they run a rallycross here? Which we did. It meant building a rallycross track, so now we have an extra gravel area. The rallycross track starts on the normal start line tarmac and heads down towards Gerards, goes through Gerards and just before you get to the Superbikes chicane it turns right onto what was grass but is now gravel. It does a zigzag and continues right the way down the run-off area adjacent to the armco the full length of the back straight until you get to just before the peeling-in point for motorcycles at Edwinas. They then rejoin the tarmac and the rallycross cars go through the Edwinas chicane, round the Esses and through the oval but once they come off the oval – instead of going down the start–finish straight where they have just started – they flick to the left, back onto the gravel and there is a gravel section that goes the full length of the start–finish straight down to the bridge where they come back onto the tarmac again. It took a fair bit of work but we managed to build it in six weeks and we ran the event a month after it was finished. That first event was in October 2009 having been approached in July. We ran a

Rallycross at Mallory Park.

Michael Groves.

second one in August 2010. We are now running a Super-Moto winter series using part of the rallycross track. So, as I said – we are becoming a motorsport centre and our geography at the centre of the country is superb.

While matters have continued smoothly at Mallory Park this has not always been the case at the Croft circuit near Darlington, as former BARC Chairman Michael Groves explains:

We knew what we were inheriting at Croft. Trevor Chaytor-Norris told us that there was litigation pending over a noise issue. We were advised by two barristers that there was little chance of action against the circuit succeeding. Eventually we ended up having to pay damages and costs. There was a further expense when we had to go to the Court of Appeal for the right to appeal. We lost that appeal.

Unfortunately, and it is a problem for all circuits, the fact that someone comes along decades after a track has opened, buys an adjacent property and then decides he or she doesn't like the noise – there is no defence in law that they must have known at the time of purchase. Noise is a nuisance by definition and it is a challenge, one that Tracey Morley at Croft has met and to her credit is turning a difficult business situation around.

Tracey takes up the story:

Below: Croft Circuit map.

When I arrived in 1997 the circuit as you see it was in the middle of being constructed. The new pits complex, offices and garages were all being built and the new track was being laid. The circuit had been dormant for a while since the late 1980s. Kate and Trevor Chaytor-Norris wanted to bring motorsport back to the North-East. They began to attract events. They reopened the circuit in 1995 and the idea was to eventually attract the top racing that was happening in the UK such as the British Touring Car Championship. Touring Cars came in 1997 along with the British Formula 3 Championship and the British GT Championships – lots of really good racing. The circuit also established itself quickly for top motorcycling racing.

Eventually being part of an estate Trevor and Kate felt that they had other interests and sought a partnership. They couldn't develop as much time and perhaps there was a financial factor – they had already put £1.5 million into redeveloping it. They felt that they needed a little bit more help. The BARC were already putting on lots of events throughout the season. That's the reason Trevor approached Dennis Carter. Trevor approached Dennis and said: 'I'm thinking of opting out because I feel it needs somebody else to run it. Taking us in a different direction and with a bit more support. Would the BARC be interested?' They took over on 1 November 2006. I had been circuit manager since 2000.

Below right: Tracey Morley.

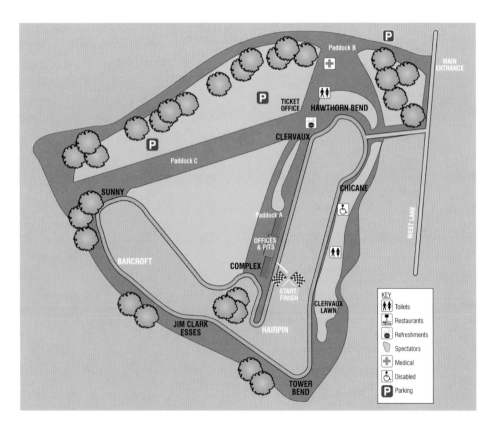

Ever since I started there have always been noise issues. At the beginning of my time we were going through a phase where we were almost getting a second planning application. The 1964 planning was fairly open – the circuit could operate unrestricted. In order to get the buildings and the redevelopment, I think it was agreed with the council that we needed to be restricted and have a different way of operating. So when I started in 1997 we were going through a unilateral undertaking – a 106 – which gave us a different planning and operating status which actually created a pyramid of noisy level days. So we had ten N1 days, forty N2 days, etc., N1 being the noisiest. We had available in that pyramid a structure that allowed 230 noisy days of different levels. The N5 was completely unrestricted. These cover events such as experience days and manufacturer days. So that's how it was and it was good.

We have a neighbour who lives just 300 metres from one of the closest points of the track. He had been trying since I arrived in 1997 to have the circuit shut down. He moved in when the circuit was already up and running – was against it – and wanted it closed. He tried all sorts of avenues – through the council, through the omsbudsman – through various channels to create problems. At the time we believed that because we had a unilateral undertaking we were guaranteed to carry on as the circuit was operating within that and nothing illegal happened. So every time he tried to have a pitch at us he was failing. Then he linked up with a solicitor who told him, 'Actually you could take a private noise nuisance out.' That's where it started and turned the corner.

In the early part of 2006 we received notification that he was bringing this private noise nuisance against us. It went into court in January 2008 for the first time and back into court in 2009 the second time and that's when we were served the injunction. The judge basically took the 230 days and said, 'I restrict you to forty.' It was a massive, massive challenge. The judge then left us with the quiet level days. Testing and lots of bike track days went by the wayside. When they served the injunction in 2009 I had to cancel ninety-four days that were booked into the calendar. It was a challenge to the business model and I think the BARC directors thought about it long and hard. Do they go forward with it or do they call it a day? They stuck with it, which was good. It would have been absolutely desperate if they had said

Above: Touring cars at Croft.

Left: British Superbikes at Croft.

Above: British Superbikes action at Croft.

no – forget about it – and pulled the plug. One, it would have meant that the neighbour would have won. Two, which is more important, there would have been no major motorsport in the North-East. I think that it is very important that we are here.

We are still prioritising. 2010 was the first year of really looking at the figures hard and saying these are the activities that make us the most profit and they are the ones that we need. Of course, trends change so it has been another look in 2011. We retain the major events – the Touring Cars and the Superbikes. There are a lot of club meetings and we have a local club – the Darlington and District Motor Club – who also support us with car meetings. Then we also have motorcycle meetings.

The hard part is developing the business again – certainly at the quiet level. The driving experience days is the area we have to progress to see if we can create a business that is profitable in order to put facilities back on the site.

Sound monitoring is vital. Prior to the injunction we had a little monitor at the appropriate place at Sunny Out – an area on the circuit where we have to monitor the noise officially for the council. We never knew what the noise levels were until we brought the monitor in at the end of the day. It was crucial to operate the business going forward after the injunction was served that we got a different system. I can see from a display monitor in my office what is happening to the noise at all times. That helps us to develop the quiet level activity. For instance we can let cars out for a certain period on the track and as soon as it gets to a certain reading we can stop it. It's a wonderful system. I think it is at the forefront of circuit technology – designed by a company one of whose directors is massively into motorsport – he raced cars. He understands our problem. He certainly wanted the circuit to work and created this. It was installed in September 2009. We would not be without it for the quiet days. It is very important. Without that system it would be really difficult to take the business forward.

Chief Executive Dennis Carter adds his perspective:

What's happened at Croft has harmed us, has hurt us but hasn't killed us. It's a real challenge, but we will survive. It just means that we have got to change the focus of the business. We are going to have two or three tough years but we will come out of it and start to build the business. I look back and Pembrey was tough. It is now a very successful part of the operation but it wasn't. I can remember having to defend Pembrey to the Council. When the majority of the Council wanted to close it down, I said, 'There will be a day when you will say thank God that we've got Pembrey!' The same situation, I believe, will happen with Croft. There is nothing in this world that won't work as long as you find the formula to make it work. Croft can't work in the way that it used to work so you change the formula and you make it work.

Meanwhile the anchor circuit of Thruxton has proved a challenge because of its limitations as the Chief Executive explained:

We are limited to twelve racing days. Thruxton is a difficult site to really make money from. We do put big events on but in the future it's going to be difficult to see how you can sustain that unless the venue has massive investment. It is active in other ways. It supports the racing school activity which we acquired in 1999. So that gives us both sides of the profit on that. It helps but it is not the complete answer for Thruxton.

Tom Jones has been circuit manager since 1994 and has seen the changes and the challenges:

F3 testing, Thruxton.

Thruxton driving experience.

Tom Jones.

The biggest change was the total resurfacing and the tunnel which we undertook in one close season. Before that we had to take vehicles across the track in gaps between races. Competitors would complain that once they had finished their race and wanted to go home – they couldn't. The tunnel made such a difference as cars could come and go. The other major work has been the upgrading of the safety facilities such as the armco and the tyre walls in my time. Overall the biggest achievement has been traffic management. There used to be long queues and this impacted on the main road. Thanks to cooperation with the police, local authority and the landowner, we are now able to bring spectators on site to various car parks and clear the area in about an hour after major events.

We suffer from being restricted to those twelve race days – not twelve meetings – twelve race days. So the British Superbikes take three of those for instance. We are limited to four test days and overall with the driving experience days we are only allowed ninety days. We still have successful manufacturer days where companies such as Mercedes can promote their range by becoming involved with local dealerships who can invite guests to come and drive on an actual circuit. However, we do need more flexibility about noise levels so that we can develop the business.

13

OTHER DEVELOPMENTS

The BARC has diverse interests embracing such things as Touring Cars, overseas consultation and a long tradition of hillclimbs. Dennis Carter adds this perspective:

Touring Cars becoming part of the empire was a two-fold matter. We always ran a third of the Touring Car events at various circuits. In those days it was divided up between BRDC, BRSSC and ourselves. I was then asked to go and talk to a chap called Alan Gow who was running Touring Cars then as he is now. He said, 'We would like you to run all of them.' I knew it was going to create a real argument in motorsport because the BRDC and the BRSCC would be very unhappy about the fact that I would come in and take charge. So I said no. For about a year we carried on running four events each.

Then I got a similar phone call a year later to go and talk to Alan Gow again so I went. He repeated, 'I want you to run all of them.' I replied, 'We had this conversation a year ago and I don't think it is the right thing.' That would have been 1998. He said, 'Well, it's your decision but if you don't then I will put my own team together to do it.' So we took it on and started to run all of the events. Then Touring Cars sold TOCA to Nicola Foulston of British Motorsports Promotions. They started to run it but began to lose a lot of money on the operation. They couldn't afford to continue to lose the amount of money that they were losing so they decided to get out. So I looked at it and said that I would take it on. We would pay off the debt in exchange for the commercial rights. They agreed. We did a contract in 2004 and took it over lock, stock and barrel. Alan Gow actually runs it from his base in Surrey. He was re-employed to look after it. He understands it. Meanwhile we do all the accounts at Thruxton.

As for overseas consultation, we have been involved in other countries. I did some marshal training in Barbados for the Barbados Motor Club, whom I got to know. We began to pick up enquiries because we had been successful in what we were doing in this country, particularly when the motorsport judicial system changed. We began to look at the way we ran our race meetings and structured our race meetings. Historically we ran the FIA system. So you have a Clerk of the Course who runs an event but any judicial matter is dealt with by the stewards of the meeting. In this country, several years ago, they changed that system so that the Clerk of the Course is also the first line of the judicial system. So the Clerk of the Course makes the first

Bottom right: Moscow road circuit.

Touring cars.

judicial decision. When that happened it was quite a change for motorsport. . . . We realised at the time that we were going to have to look very carefully at how we structured race meetings, how we organised race meetings and particularly how we put the team together to operate race meetings. We seemed to get that right. The way we were doing it really seemed to work and everybody was starting to follow the way that we were doing it. That gave us a bit of a kickstart into training other people. So we had done various bits and pieces.

I had also been to look to do some work in Russia. That goes back to 1988 and 1989 when we were looking to run a race in Moscow. It was a street circuit. It was going to be very much like the Birmingham Super Prix. So we got involved in that and employed a guy called Frank Flower who had been the sponsorship manager for Shell – responsible for the British Grand Prix when Shell were sponsoring it. Frank was our man in Moscow! We got a long way down the road. We had support from Tim Jackson of Renault who were going to provide the support races.

MOSCOW RIVER

PADDOCK RETURN ROAD

FINISH   START

PIT LANE

LIGHTS CONSIDERED EXIT

CIRCUIT LENGTH APPROX 2.7 Km

MAP SCALE 1:333

MOSCOW STATE UNIVERSITY

RACE CONTROL & TIMEKEEPING

PADDOCK 2   PADDOCK 1

A sticker from the Russian initiative.

It was effectively going to be a Formula 3 race on the streets of Moscow supported by the Renault categories. Tim and I went back and forth to Moscow quite a bit. Then we did a launch in London and went to Moscow for a launch the same day. Everything was in place. Then we had the tanks on the streets episode and somebody got killed. Our sponsor – who happened to be American – said that they couldn't get involved in anything like this in Russia and they backed out. That killed the event unfortunately. The circuit that we designed was used quite a few times and as far as I know may still be. It was just a little street circuit in front of the University building up on the hill. It was in an interesting part of Moscow because it was where the ski slopes started for the Moscow Olympics.

Then we got involved in Dubai. To a large extent we pointed the personnel at Dubai. The Dubai project was on-going and they were looking for staff so we recommended some people to go and work there. In turn they brought us in to do a lot of their training work. So that obviously worked really well for us. After Dubai we got the Abu Dhabi contract to help them out with their first Grand Prix. We are actually out of contract on all of them but we still work in Dubai. We got involved in India because we were asked to do some work for Pakistan. The present President of Pakistani Motorsport was President of the Bahrain and Saudi Arabian Federation. I got to know him and we had done a job in Bahrain. I had met him in 2006 but Dubai goes back before that. Our first ever event in Dubai was F1 GTs and we did A1GP, GP2 and a 24-hour race which we are still doing with them. The Abu Dhabi Grand Prix is the most recent high-profile event. The first year we took 360 people out there to work alongside their people and train their people. It's the way this whole thing works really. You go into these arrangements knowing that you are doing yourself out of work, that you are training them to do it themselves. It will be the same in India.

We are talking to a couple of other countries about doing work for them. Most of our work has been away from F1. Abu Dhabi was really the first F1 we did directly. We have been involved in preparing people to do Formula 1, but not directly. It has always been: you will need to do this and this and this – and then you will eventually build up to that. We enjoy the whole training and it has been very good

Abu Dhabi.

Right: BARC marshals in Abu Dhabi.

Below left: Harewood Hill, 1968, PR2 Ford S.C. 1,650cc.

Below centre: Austin Healey Sprite at Harewood Hill, 1968.

Below right: Through the Farmhouse at Harewood Hill.

for us as a club. We have probably taken five or six hundred different British marshals to work events. These are voluntary but obviously we pay to get them there and back while looking after them when we are there. Motorsport could not operate without its voluntary input.

We are talking to new countries the whole time. British motorsport has a positive image and the BARC has a reputation for very good organisation.

Back home the hillclimbs are a very important part of the BARC because it is a lower form of motorsport that we are into. They are very much run by the centres, Gurston by the South-Western and Harewood by the Yorkshire Centre. They are very important to us in terms of what they do. We are fortunate in that being a club as opposed to being a straight commercial organisation – we can take a view on matters. We have been able to develop the two hillclimb clubs because we don't need a direct financial return as a commercial operator would. You are never going to pour money down a drain but you can take a rather more benevolent view of matters. We have been able to develop both Gurston and Harewood fairly slowly but they have both developed quite well. Harewood we have lengthened and we have put new buildings in at both. We have gradually moved the standards of the venues up. Typical BARC because we don't fit the mould – I think that I'm right in saying that they are the only two hillclimbs in the country that start going downhill!

Karousel Bend at Gurston Down in 1968.

The BARC's experience with hillclimbs was shown in a positive light when the Motor Sports Association announced in July 2011 that they had been appointed to promote the MSA British Hill Climb Championship and Hill Climb Leaders Championship for a period of five years from 1 January 2012. What an appropriate way to start their centenary year.

Dennis Carter's insight

Sidecars at Gurston Down, 1968.

We were delighted to have been given this opportunity. When Tony Fletcher first suggested that we should apply to run the championships when he decided to retire, we were flattered to say the least. Tony has done a great job in keeping the championships strong and healthy and will be a hard act to follow. However, in asking Tim Wilson – a competitor himself – and his wife Jackie to look after the championships on our behalf and with the strength of the BARC behind them we are confident that we can continue the good work. The championships will remain unchanged for 2012 and we look forward to working with competitors and organising clubs to develop them thereafter.

14

GOODWOOD REVIVED

Freddie March had handed over the running of the Goodwood Estate to his son in 1968. The motor racing circuit was not a priority and he could easily have let it fall into disuse. Despite his relative lack of interest in motor racing, he nevertheless continued to maintain the motor circuit throughout the 1970s and 1980s. Otherwise the revival of the circuit could never have happened.

In the early 1990s the duke, in turn, passed the running of the Goodwood Estate to his son – the present Lord March. Charles March had been deeply influenced by his grandfather. During Easter school holidays, Charles had stayed at Goodwood absorbing Freddie's love for and knowledge of motor racing and meeting the great drivers of the 1960s.

When his father retired, Charles set about creating the Goodwood Festival of Speed, first run in 1993. It was an instant success. Every year since, the festival as grown in stature to become the largest event of its kind in the world. This came from a number of people proposing some kind of motoring event. For instance Ian Bax of the BARC suggested a hillclimb on the estate roads adjacent to Goodwood House. The RAC Motor Sports Association approved and so Charles March drew together a team of experts and an outline began to take shape based around the concept of great historic and contemporary cars and motorcycles tackling a hillclimb running from the estate's East Gates, past the front of Goodwood House and up the hill beyond. The organising team pursued a conscious desire to offer an alternative to modern motor racing which excludes rather than includes the fans. At the Festival of Speed enthusiasts found themselves with access to both cars and drivers.

Once the festival had been established, it was perhaps predictable that Charles March would nurture plans for the circuit. With continuous use the surface of the track had been maintained and the main safety measures were in place. Derek Ongaro, the MSA's circuit inspector, suggested modifications but was persuaded that Goodwood's unique feature was as the only circuit in the world to remain unaltered since 1952. Derek agreed, subject to the proviso that racing was restricted to cars built no later than 1972. One problem was the decibel limits imposed in 1985 under a Noise Abatement Notice. The result was the creation of a large

Lord March in his office.

earth banks which together with the planting of trees and shrubs were designed to absorb and deflect noise. Goodwood negotiated with the local council who finally accepted a proposal to allow five days of unsilenced historic racing. In December 1996 the council referred its decision to the Department of the Environment for potential review. A swift but favourable response meant that an opening date in September 1998 – fifty years after the first ever meeting – was an achievable target.

As stated, some of the work had already been undertaken prior to the planning application. Now there was impetus for everything to be put into operation. The BARC became involved with Dennis Carter as an advisor to the project. It was decided that preference would be given to drivers and cars with a Goodwood connection. This meant a cut-off point of 1966. Formula Junior and the 500cc Formula 3 were essential, as were handicaps. Both Members' Meetings and internationals would have to be represented as well as such landmark events as the Nine Hours Race and the Tourist Trophy.

On 18 September 1948, Frederick, the 9th Duke of Richmond and Gordon had driven his new Bristol 400 to open the Goodwood circuit. Fifty years later, to the day, his grandson, Charles the Earl of March, drove an identical car around the circuit and declared it reopened. Practice all day Friday and on the Saturday morning preceded four races on the Saturday afternoon with eight more on Sunday.

First race on the programme after thirty-two years' absence was the Woodcote Cup for Formula 1, 2, and Libre cars of the type which raced at Goodwood until 1953. Ludovic Lindsay stormed into the lead in what had been his late father Patrick's ex-Bira ERA 'Remus'. He eventually became Goodwood's first motor race winner since 1966. Less than a second covered the first three with the Cooper-Bristols of Roddy MacPherson and Gregor Fisken in hot pursuit.

It turned out to be an amazing weekend and so much more than just an historic race meeting. As Murray Walker testifies:

I cannot find words strong enough for what Charles March has done. He has created two events in the Revival and the Festival which by a very considerable margin are the best of their kind in the whole world. They are literally absolutely unique. Two very different events. One is a sort of high-speed demonstration up the hill in front of the house. The other is balls-out racing on a proper circuit which he has restored to perfection and as it was when it closed. Not as it would be nowadays with armco and run-off areas. You have to be tremendously determined and forthright to do what he has done. I used to be slightly tongue-in-cheek, but not all that much, and say that I would willingly give up all the Grand Prix for the two Goodwood meetings. That's what I think of them. My one regret is that I missed the first. I was doing a hell of a lot of travelling at the time and was home very little. They were hoping for 5,000 and they got 25,000. It has grown and now they've got the motor

show there as well. Charles is not just a motorsport enthusiast – he's got a very fertile, creative mind. He started his career as a photographer. He is a gigantically tough and talented businessman who has created two events where people who own veteran, vintage and historic cars – no matter where they are in the world – are almost literally vying with each other for the privilege of being able to go there with their cars. It's incredible. The whole scene with such as the spivs. Some bloke coming up with a long coat and asking, 'Want to buy a watch guv?' with the whole of the inside of the coat covered in watches.

John Surtees has been involved in recent years:

Charles March asked me back in 2010 for a Surtees parade of bikes and cars. In a sense the modern events are a little more managed than the race era. They have to be to create their own character. The festival is different from the revival. The festival is more open and fans can get close. It's a big garden party really. The revival is more serious as it does involve racing. There are good cars and a mixture of competitors from the past and present. The ladies like the dress code. Thanks to the BARC the

Above left: Rowan Atkinson as Mr Bean.

Above centre: Sir Stirling Moss.

Above right: Carnaby Street recreated.

157

events are relaxed but efficient, a time to meet old friends and make new ones. I had three cars that had just been stored on parade. The first F1 car from Team Surtees, a championship F2 car and another F2 car.

Sir Stirling Moss is a fan too:

I very much enjoy going back there for the revival meeting and the festival. It has a great atmosphere and the circuit is now as it was before. It has a massive public attendance and I like the way people make the effort to dress up to recapture a past era. I've driven various cars there in recent years too.

Sir Jackie Stewart shares this enthusiasm:

A Talbot Darracq at the Goodwood Festival.

I am so pleased about the revival meetings there these days. It is one of my favourite events in the diary. They make so much effort. For example, dressing up in pre-1966 clothing. Lord March and the BARC have done so well with it.

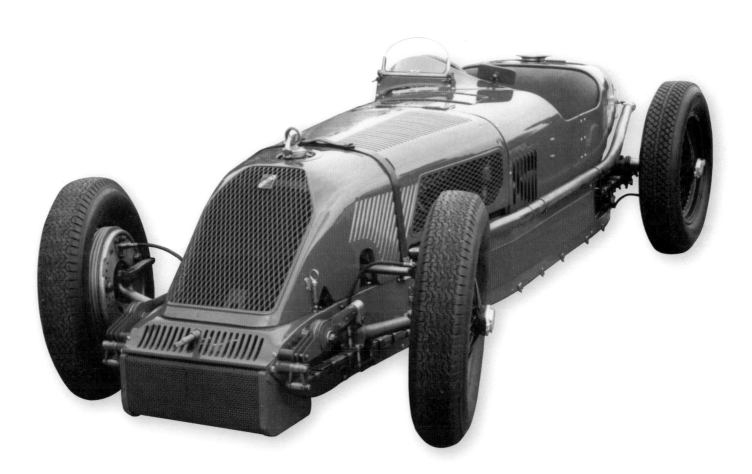

Above: A Mercedes Benz 300SL Roadster at the Goodwood Festival.

Right: Bugatti T35.

Far right: A Maserati at the Goodwood Festival.

159

Thrust SSC at the 1996 Goodwood Festival.

15

THE BARC IN PERSPECTIVE

MICHAEL GROVES, PAST CHAIRMAN

I'm lucky that Sidney Offord, Dennis Carter and myself always got on well and worked together. Plus the Council have always been so supportive. Council members come and go through retirement and election but we have always been in agreement. We have always pulled together and that has made the club strong.

There are disagreements before policy is decided but that is healthy. We never go home bad-tempered or not friends. That's rare as most clubs of any description tend to be riddled with arguments. The BARC is not.

MURRAY WALKER OBE

To say that the BARC is one of the very few leading motorsport organisations in this country is a masterpiece of understatement. It has done an absolutely fantastic job and it has had some great personalities. People like Sid Offord – irascible, loveable, demanding, great fun.

The BARC do a fabulous social job with their members in terms of all the material that Trevor Swettenham puts out with the magazine and the big night out – the dinner that they have every year. Not all the clubs are good at that. The BARC is a big club with over 4,000 members. A very strong social side with all the regional centres.

Some outstanding people – not the least of whom is Dennis Carter. Big, bluff and very vigorous.

SIR STIRLING MOSS

They do a very good job. I've been familiar with them since the days when John Morgan was involved. They are an outstanding motorsport organisation whom I advise people to join. I've received two gold medals from them in my career and they have pride of place in Lady Susan's study.

SIR JACKIE STEWART

I received a gold medal from them. It is framed alongside my six BRDC gold stars and hangs proudly in my well-stocked loo at home! It is the visitors' loo actually, so they can share in my happy memories.

The BARC is well-recognised, well-respected and an important part of British motorsport history.

JOHN SURTEES OBE, MBE

The BARC are a vital part of British motorsport, particularly junior motorsport, which has largely relied on the BARC for many of the formulae. They are resurrecting another starter formula. They are setting up a new formula using BMW cars: in a sense an alternative to Formula Ford, but using a winged car. They are important to young drivers and their development. When I was on the board of the BRDC, I would have liked to have seen a greater degree of cooperation between the clubs that ran circuits. It was left to the BARC to promote the grassroots. All strength to them. Generally, the BARC has done a very worthwhile and creditable job.

DR JONATHAN PALMER

As Chief Executive of MSV I now have quite a bit to do with the BARC once again. Like MSV, BARC operates four circuits so Chief Executive Dennis Carter and I have a close working relationship and share a rare insight into the challenges of running circuits, such as commercial, environmental and safety issues. It is not an easy business! Though our club MSVR, we also run motor racing championships, like the BARC.

The BARC has been a major part of British motorsport for many decades, has achieved great success and I'm sure will continue to be an important organisation in national motorsport.

Appendix

BARC GOLD MEDAL RECIPIENTS

The BARC's Gold Medal is awarded by the Council of the BARC 'for outstanding achievement in motor racing by British subjects'. This is not an annual award and is given only when the Council of the BARC considers it is merited.

Gold Medal Recipients:

Year	Name	Achievement
1955	Stirling Moss	British GP and Mille Miglia
1957	David Murray	Ecurie Ecosse Le Mans Victory
1958	Mike Hawthorn	World Championship of Drivers
1959	Sir David Brown	Aston Martin – Constructors' World Sports Car Championship
1959	John Cooper	Cooper – Constructors' World Championship F1 and F2
1959	Jack Brabham	World Championship of Drivers
1960	Pat Moss and Ann Wisdom	European Ladies Rally Championship
1961	Stirling Moss	Monaco and German Grand Prix
1962	Graham Hill	World Championship of Drivers
1962	Sir Alfred Owen	BRM-F1 Constructors' World Championship
1963	Jim Clark	World Championship of Drivers
1964	John Surtees	World Championship of Drivers
1965	Jim Clark	Indianapolis 500 Winner
1965	Colin Chapman	Lotus 35 Indianapolis Constructor
1966	Jack Brabham	World Championships, Drivers and F1 Constructors
1967	Jack Brabham	Brabham – F1 Constructors' World Championship
1967	Denny Hulme	World Championship of Drivers
1968	Jim Clark	25 Grand Prix wins

Sir Jack Brabham receives his Gold Medal in 1959.

1968	Graham Hill	World Championship of Drivers
1969	John Wyer	Gulf Ford Le Mans wins 1968 and 1969
1971	Jackie Stewart	World Championship of Drivers
1971	Ken Tyrrell	Tyrrell – F1 Constructors' World Championship
1972	Graham Hill	First driver to win a World Championship, Le Mans and the Indianapolis 500
1973	Colin Chapman	50 Lotus Grand Prix wins
1973	Jackie Stewart	26 Grand Prix wins
1975	Lord Alexander Hesketh	Outstanding contribution to motor racing
1976	James Hunt	World Championship of Drivers
1978	Colin Chapman	Lotus – F1 Constructors' World Championship
1980	Brian Henton	European Formula 2 Championship
1983	Dr Jonathan Palmer	European Formula 2 Championship
1985	Derek Bell	World Endurance Championship
1986	Frank Williams	Williams – F1 Constructors' World Championship
1987	Sidney Offord	For outstanding services – BARC Executive Director for 15 years
1987	Jaguar Cars	World Sports Prototype Championship
1988	Ron Dennis	McLaren – F1 Constructors' World Championship
1988	Martin Brundle	World Sports Prototype Championship
1990	Nigel Mansell	Equalling the highest number of Grand Prix wins by an English driver
1992	Nigel Mansell	FIA F1 World Championship of Drivers
1992	Patrick Head and Adrian Newey	For design of FIA F1 World Championship-winning Williams Renault FW 14B
1992	Derek Warwick	FIA Sportscar World Championship
1996	Murray Walker	For his outstanding service to motor racing
1996	Damon Hill	FIA F1 World Championship of Drivers
1998	Ken Tyrrell	In recognition of a lifetime's involvement in British motorsport
2002	Gerry Marshall	In recognition of his outstanding contribution to British motorsport
2006	Andy Priaulx	In recognition of his 2005 World Touring Car Championship success
2007	Tom Wheatcroft	In recognition of his outstanding contribution to British motorsport
2008	Andy Priaulx	In recognition of three successive World Touring Car Championship successes
2009	Ron Dennis	In recognition of McLaren's success in F1 racing with Lewis Hamilton and his commitment to driver development
2009	Lewis Hamilton	FIA F1 World Championship of Drivers
2009	Michael Groves	To mark 30 years as Chairman of BARC Ltd and to acknowledge his unstinting contribution to the club.
2010	Jenson Button	FIA F1 World Championship of Drivers
2010	Ross Brawn	FIA F1 Constructors' Championship

Sir Jackie Stewart, who won his first Gold Medal in 1971.

BIBLIOGRAPHY

Bagnall, Tony, *The Unfulfilled Dream: The Story of Motor Racing at Aintree*, TFM Publishing.
Collins, S.S., *Motor Racing at Crystal Palace*, Veloce Publishing.
Lawrence, Mike, Taylor, Simon and Nye, Doug, *The Glory of Goodwood*, Virgin Publishing.
Parfitt, Philip, *Racing at Crystal Palace*, Motor Racing Publications Ltd.
Rogers, Gareth, *Mallory Park: Fifty Years at the Friendly Circuit*, Tempus Publishing.
Walkerley, Rodney, *Brooklands to Goodwood*, G.T. Foulis & Co. Ltd.

PHOTOGRAPHY

BARC archive, Thruxton circuit
BARC – Ontario, Canada
Brooklands Library
Pete Gibson
Nick Gladwin
Grace's Guide
Bruce Grant-Braham
Goodwood Photo Library
Renault F1
Colin Shipway
Trevor Swettenham
Thruxton Racing School
Tony Todd
John Ward

ACKNOWLEDGEMENTS

The author would like to thank the following for their assistance in the preparation of this book and additional material:

Mike Ashcroft (Aintree Circuit Club)
John Bailie (Aintree Circuit Club)
Colin Billings (Sevenoaks Motor Club)
Marion Calver-Smith (Goodwood)
Clive Cooke
Mandy Curley
Nan Einarson (BARC – Ontario, Canada)
Amy Harrison (BARC – Ontario, Canada)
Andrew Hext (Gurston Down)
Rupert Lloyd Thomas
Simon McBeath (Gurston Down)
Sir Stirling Moss
Dr Jonathan Palmer
John Pulford (Brooklands)
Brian Robinson
Phil Rogers
Sir Jackie Stewart
John Surtees
Andrew Tweedie (www.GraciesGuides.co.uk)
Murray Walker
Ian Watson
Ellen Westbrook (Goodwood Photo Library)

With special thanks to the former BARC archivist Enid Smith for her efficient organisation of the photo collection at Thruxton and to the BARC Press Officer Trevor Swettenham for his consistent input and support.

Index